BEST OF TEACHER-TO-TEACHER

The Ultimate Beginner's Guide

NEA Teacher-to-Teacher Books

Copyright © 2000

National Education Association of the United States

Printing History

First Printing: June 2000

NOTE: The opinions expressed in this book should not be construed as representing the policy or position of the National Education Association. Materials published by the NEA Professional Library are intended to be discussion documents for educators who are concerned with specialized interests of the profession.

CREDITS: *Series Editor:* Sabrina Holcomb. *Contributing Editors:* Marina Michalski and Julie Leupold. *Cover and Book Design:* Catherine Rawson, Sue Nixson, and Hallie Shell. *Series Design:* NoBul Graphics.

This book is printed on acid free paper. This book is printed with soy ink.

Library of Congress Cataloging-in-Publication Data

Best of teacher-to-teacher: the ultimate beginner's guide.
    p. cm.—(Teacher-to-teacher series)
"NEA teacher-to-teacher books."
Consists of excerpts from books published in the Teacher-to-teacher series.
Includes bibliographical references (p.).
ISBN 0-8106-2917-8
    1. Teaching—United States. I. Teacher-to-teacher series. II. Series.

LB1775.2 .B48 2000
371.102—dc21
    00-034649

Contents

5 — How To Use This Book

6 — Introduction

9 — Having a Great Day at Chickasha
By Jana Dabney, Sharon Wilson, Rita Cavin, and Vickie Holloway
Chickasha Intermediate School in Chickasha, Oklahoma, was known for its discipline problems and plunging morale. This is the story of how a teaching staff developed discipline initiatives that turned the school around.

23 — Engaging Hard-to-Reach Parents
By Theresa Abernethy and Laura Lavin
Community outreach programs and parenting workshops helped educators at Teachers Memorial School break through the barrier of parent mistrust.

37 — Creating Critical Thinkers
By Eileen Moreno
This third grade teacher used a thematic unit on change to challenge her third graders to use higher level thinking skills. In the process, she formed important links between academic subjects and adhered to district curriculum requirements.

49 — Community Treasure Hunt
By Joan Reid
A second grade teacher in Harrison, Arkansas, discovered a treasure trove of free resources in her own "backyard." She shares her methods for canvassing the local business community, soliciting donations, and using parents as a resource to get free supplies for her classroom.

63 — Weathering Multiple Intelligences
By Barbara Kendall and Shirley Harless
These teachers created a thematic unit on weather, complete with learning activities that corresponded to each of the seven areas of intelligence.

75 — Wired for Better Writing
By Beth Cristensen
This middle school teacher wanted to give her traditional English lessons a new-tech twist. Now she oversees a classroom of eighth-grade authors whose Web writing enjoys an international audience.

89 — Using the Present To Teach the Past
By Carol Steele
This high school teacher bridged the gap between young and old with an oral history project. No textbook could match the learning students gained from interviews with their elderly neighbors.

101 — Sharing the Wealth
By Ellie Hanlon, Jennifer Curtis, and Lori Goodine
Veteran teachers in Weymouth, Massachusetts, share their wisdom and experience with newcomers through a Share the Wealth mentoring program, created by the Weymouth Teachers Association.

115 — Selected Resources

How To Use this Book

Best of Teacher: The Ultimate Beginner's Guide is no ordinary book. It is one of NEA's Teacher-to-Teacher Books, in which classroom and resource teachers speak directly to other teachers—like you—about their efforts to improve the quality of teaching and learning.

Printed in the upper right-hand corner of every book in the series is a routing slip that encourages you to pass the book on to colleagues once you've read it—in other words, to spread the word about school change.

Previous topics in the series have covered the following areas: large-scale school change, student assessment, multi-age grouping, integrated thematic teaching, parent involvement, inclusion, innovative discipline, multiple intelligences, technology for diverse learners, how to get grants and free resources, peer mentoring, and integrating technology into the curriculum.

Read the Six Stories

Inside this book you'll find stories from eight or more teachers across the country. Each story illustrates step-by-step how they tackled a specific restructuring challenge. They describe what worked and didn't work in the process. Each chapter includes diagrams, checklists, or tables you can use in your efforts to develop, facilitate, or improve similar programs in your district.

Reader Reflections

At the end of each chapter, you can jot down your immediate thoughts and ideas to follow up on in our Reader Reflections page.

You see, the purpose of Teacher-to-Teacher Books is not only to spread the word about school change but to encourage other teachers to participate in its exploration.

Discuss Your Thoughts with Others

Once you've routed a book through your school, you can meet with colleagues who contributed to the Reader Reflections sections and expand upon your thoughts.

Go Online

The communication and sharing does not have to stop there. Visit the NEA home page on the World Wide Web, your gateway to resources and information that can help you improve teaching and learning in your school. You can find us at (http://www.nea.org). From there, the Professional Library Web site is just a click away.

Introduction

Welcome to the profession that makes all other professions possible! You're embarking on a career that's exciting and challenging, and the fact that you've chosen to be a teacher says a lot about the kind of person you are.

Perhaps the most defining characteristic of people entering the teaching profession is a unique brand of pragmatic idealism. Teachers have a real desire to do some good in the world. They realize that a teacher's dedication, enthusiasm, and genuine concern have the power to change the course of a student's life.

Over the next decade, two million new teachers are expected to join America's work force. Yet many of these beginners feel that the training they've received has not prepared them for the demands of today's real-world classrooms. In addition to ageless issues such as classroom management and student discipline, they face a number of contemporary challenges, such as the demand for high-stakes testing and greater accountability, the growing number of students from widely diverse backgrounds and cultures, and the inclusion of special-needs students in general education classrooms.

As new teachers tackle these challenges, they often find that veteran teachers are their most valuable resource. These seasoned practitioners are in the trenches every day. They've asked the same questions and faced the same dilemmas as the teachers who are just starting out.

The mentoring role that veterans play in the lives of new teachers was our inspiration for this special edition of Teacher-to-Teacher. We asked beginning teachers across the country to read our most popular Teacher-to-Teacher books and choose the stories they thought would most help their colleagues. Selections on peer support, discipline, and parental involvement are just some of the chapters our readers chose as invaluable sources of practical ideas for beginners. Each selection begins with an introduction from a reader explaining how this information can help new teachers get off to a good start.

Innovative Discipline
"Having a Great Day at Chickasha"

In the past, Chickasha Intermediate was a school with a "bad rep." It was known throughout the county as a school with severe discipline problems and plunging morale, until one day the staff got together and developed a package of discipline initiatives that turned this school into a happy, welcoming place to learn.

Building Parent Partnerships
"Engaging Hard-to-Reach Parents"

In Kinston, North Carolina, educators provided parents with

transportation and child care so they could attend important school events. The school even took parents on a faculty retreat to hear their needs firsthand.

Integrated Thematic Teaching
"Creating Critical Thinkers"
Thematic units often explore big concepts and large issues that encourage students to develop higher-level thinking skills. A third grade teacher illustrates how a thematic unit on "Change" spurred thought-provoking discussions in her classroom.

How To Get Grants and Free Stuff
"Community Treasure Hunt"
Arkansas teacher Joan Reid and her colleagues at Skyline Heights Elementary School have received hundreds of free products and services from local businesses—by simply asking for them. She gives tips on using parents as resources for free materials and offers advice on soliciting free donations from community businesses.

Multiple Intelligences
"Weathering Multiple Intelligences"
Two teachers team up to add multiple intelligences activities to an integrated thematic unit on weather.

Teaching with Technology
"Wired for Better Writing"
English teacher Beth Cristensen was once terrified of computers. Now she and her eighth grade class have an award-winning Web site with an international audience. Cristensen describes the multimedia projects she uses to give traditional English lessons a new-tech twist.

Beyond Textbooks: Hands-On Learning
"Using the Present To Teach the Past"
Carol Steele, a history teacher at Union High School in Grand Rapids, Michigan, wanted a more authentic approach to teaching history. She wanted to show her students that not all history is learned from textbooks. As a result of Steele's ingenuity, students learned history from the greatest experts of all—those who lived it.

Peer Mentoring
"Sharing the Wealth"
A step-by-step illustration of how the Weymouth Teachers Association built a district-wide mentoring program, matching new teachers with experienced colleagues in their school. Teachers also meet off-site once a month for workshops and lesson-plan swaps.

Whether you're a veteran in search of innovative classroom strategies or a teacher new to the profession, you'll find that this handy guide makes a great addition to your classroom—and your career.

—Sabrina Holcomb
   Series Editor

Teacher Review

Innovative Discipline

HAVING A GREAT DAY AT CHICKASHA

One of the hardest parts in making the transition from student to teacher can be defining one's own classroom management style. Every class is different and brings with it various challenges. That's why "Having a Great Day at Chikasha" really hit home for me.

The teachers of Chikasha Intermediate School provide valuable insight and practical examples that new educators can actually use in the classroom. I found Jana Dabney's list of class rules humorous, but at the same time, they sparked ideas that I could apply to my own class rules. The ideas presented on maintaining control during cooperative learning activities are great for any teacher, especially since this tends to be a period during the school day when problems can arise if things are not handled the right way.

It's important to keep in mind that the key to making one's class run smoothly is to be consistent and fair to all students. Most of the time, the children's knowledge that they are cared for and that their teachers have a vested interest in their success equates to a minimal amount of problems. Mutual respect for all is vital to providing an equitable and caring environment for the students. Communication between teachers and parents should be frequent and positive in order to ensure fair, effective classroom discipline. In turn, this will help to build a support system at home that will reinforce school programs.

Stephanie Urlage
4th Grade Science Teacher
White Hall Elementary School
Richmond, Kentucky

HAVING A GREAT DAY AT CHICKASHA

These management strategies have led to happy students, teachers, and parents at Chickasha Intermediate School in Oklahoma.

1 The hardest part of teaching school is, undeniably, classroom management. We should know. As three classroom teachers and a principal at Chickasha Intermediate School in Chickasha, Oklahoma, we deal on a daily basis with situations requiring discipline.

Currently, our school has 479 sixth and seventh graders. Jana Dabney teaches sixth and seventh grade reading. Sharon Wilson teaches sixth and seventh grade math and serves one period each day in our ISS/SCC class (In-School-Suspension/Self-Contained Classroom). Rita Cavin teaches seventh grade geography and English. Vickie Holloway is the principal.

Five years ago, when Sharon and Vickie first arrived at Chickasha Intermediate, we were a school with severe discipline problems and plunging morale. As Jana reflects, "What concerned me most at the time, was not the 380 students acting out,

JANA DABNEY
Sixth and Seventh Grade Reading
SHARON WILSON
Sixth and Seventh Grade Math
RITA CAVIN
Seventh Grade Geography and English
VICKIE HOLLOWAY
Principal
Chickasha Intermediate School
Chickasha, Oklahoma

but the 30 adults who stood by and let it happen." In many cases, teachers had become afraid of the students; in other cases, they felt overwhelmed by the number of problems and began to let things slide.

Many parents were concerned about the situation. Some have mentioned since that they considered home schooling as an alternative to sending their child to Intermediate.

Things have changed in the last five years, however. Not long after Vickie and Sharon came to Intermediate, our staff

THE ULTIMATE BEGINNER'S GUIDE

decided that in order to succeed, we had to come together as a team. It took a lot of patience, planning, and hard work, but today, we are a school that operates on two key words: *pride* and *respect*.

This is the story of how our staff developed both schoolwide and individual classroom management initiatives that turned our school around.

This is the story of how our staff developed both schoolwide and individual classroom management initiatives that turned our school around.

It is also the story of how we continue to work daily on providing a nurturing atmosphere and on rewarding positive behavior in order to ensure an appropriate working environment for our students and for ourselves.

Schoolwide Initiatives

Our first experience as a team was to meet and design a set of strategies to control student behavior. As we worked together, our mission evolved— Success for All, Now and Tomorrow.

Early Morning Structure

We decided that our first priority was to get students ready to learn each morning. The morning playground had been chaotic with fights and with students running wild, not paying attention to the directives of the playground supervisor, and generally coming into the school too wired to effectively participate in classroom activities.

The dean of students suggested that we place all students in a structured environment each morning. We decided that as students came to school in the morning, they would take a seat in our rarely used auditorium where they could do homework or read. We also decided that the principal, dean of students, and counselor would greet every student each morning as he or she came into the auditorium. They would send students who were upset, or who for some other reason were not ready to learn, to talk with one of the staff immediately.

This has proved to be effective, and we have increased its effectiveness by having students sit in homeroom groups and by conducting two DEAR (Drop Everything and Read) sessions a week during this time.

Prior to dismissal from the auditorium each morning, students are instructed to sit up straight and pay attention to the speaker. At this time, a staff member goes over any upcoming events or school problems. (People who come to our assemblies are always in awe of our students' behavior during assemblies.)

Homogeneous Grouping

Our next project was to examine the effectiveness of our developmental classes, which tended to be a breeding ground for discipline problems. Two teachers agreed not to level their classes for all subjects except math, and to use only high/low grouping there. At the end of the year, they found teaching without the developmental classes to be much easier on classroom management and more academically successful for students in general. Their testimony convinced the other teachers to discontinue developmental classes.

Reward Systems

Around December of that first year, we also decided to reward children for being just plain ole good kids. Vickie contacted one of our industrious parents who organized volunteers to bring ice cream and toppings to school. This was our first attempt to recognize good behavior.

Our Parent-Teachers Organization now conducts a "Positive Incentive Program" every semester in which students who meet the behavioral criteria are rewarded with a party. Here are the criteria: (1) students must have less than three tardies per nine weeks, (2) their record must not show an office referral because of severe behavior problems, and (3) they may not receive more than three teacher-assigned detentions. Last semester, 356 out of 444 students attended the party.

In one of our trying times, we started the "Three Strikes and You're Out" project. Here's how that works: Approximately three weeks before a special event, we announce to the students that the plan is beginning. Each hour, teachers keep track of students who exhibit improper behavior. At the end of the day, the office randomly calls for the strikes given during certain hours (i.e., "Send down the names of persons receiving strikes in second, fifth, and sixth periods."). Each person listed receives one strike. If a student receives three strikes before the day of the special event, he or she may not attend. Along the way, we have adopted a few exceptions to the three-strikes process such as: "A student cannot strike out during one hour," and "A substitute's strikes are not counted." (The students do not know this one!)

Parent Shadowing

One of our teachers shared the idea of parent shadowing with us. In this activity, the parent of a disruptive child comes to school and follows the child through the school day. This has proved to be very effective. Rarely have we had to use this technique more than once with a student! (Principal shadowing works well, too.)

Self-Contained Classroom

Time and time again, it came to us that we have many, many good students. It's just that a group you can count on both hands makes it seem like behavior is out of control.

For these students, we initiated a Self-Contained Classroom (SCC) in which they receive personalized instruction in core academic classes. We also teach these students basic social skills such as how to play

> **More About Chickasha**
>
> Chickasha is a county-seat community of about 16,000 people, located in central Oklahoma. The economic base of the surrounding county is predominantly agricultural and oil-related. In Chickasha, light industry is the chief source of jobs. The population is diverse in race, education, and social status. About 60 percent of the work force is employed in blue-collar labor. About a fourth of the work force is professional. The population is relatively mobile. Fifty percent of the families are comprised of a single parent or a stepparent.

a game without cheating or fighting.

The room for SCC has a sink and rest room facilities. Students with good behavior who are in SCC are allowed to go out into the hall between classes to use the rest room and cafeteria and to go to electives. If their behavior has not been appropriate, the class becomes completely self-contained, and they are required to

The beginning of the year is extremely important to successful classroom management.

use the rest room facilities within the classroom. Even lunch is brought in to them. As students' behavior and attitude improve, they are placed back, one or two courses at a time, into a regular classroom setup.

We developed a multi-criteria instrument to determine who needed to be in this program. Out of 11 students in the program last year, some were eventually referred to day treatment programs, but we also had three stars. These stars made the program worth it. One former SCC student even became a National Junior Honor Society member.

Individual Initiatives

Teachers at Chickasha Intermediate have developed a number of discipline strategies independent of one another as well. Following are first-person reports from Jana, Sharon, and Rita on some of their personal classroom management techniques.

Jana Dabney's Classroom Initiatives

It has always intrigued me that discipline is what we classroom teachers are professionally judged and evaluated by, yet it is something we receive very little professional training in. For the most part, we receive our lessons in this area from the "School of Hard Knocks" and/or "Experience U."

One thing I have learned from this personal experience is that the beginning of the year is extremely important to successful classroom management. This is when you establish your particular style of organization. How you handle this time can determine how the rest of the year goes. Some concepts associated with implementing effective classroom management are

- establishing workable rules and procedures,
- giving adequate explanations for rules and procedures, and
- establishing your role as the classroom leader.

Rules To Work By

When I started my first job as a junior high math teacher (my sixth year of teaching experience), one of my new colleagues, in an attempt to show me the ropes, shared a list of official classroom rules that I was to use in my room. There were so many rules, it took all of one side of the paper and half of the other just to list them! I was really sick. It seemed I had been hired more as a detective/police officer than as the math teacher. After several attempts to absorb this highly complex document, I finally sat down and wrote a succinct list of behaviors that I simply couldn't tolerate in my classroom. My own rules to work by evolved from this list. To this day, I review them with all of my students when they first enter my classroom. I then post the list in a prominent place for the remainder of the year.

Mrs. Dabney's Classroom Rules

- *If Mrs. Dabney is talking, DON'T!*
- *If assigned, do it (on time, with a smile)!*
- *If you don't want to do it over, do it right the first time!*
- *If it's a school rule, follow it!*
- *If you are supposed to have it, be sure you do EVERY DAY!*
- *If allowed time to work in class, use it wisely!*
- *If you gripe about the assignment, be prepared to do extra!*
- *If you are angry, bite the bullet!*

Following is how I explain these rules to my students:

- *If Mrs. Dabney is talking, DON'T!* (Unfortunately, I talk a lot, so don't even plan on much talking at all!)

- *If assigned, do it on time and with a smile!* (Keep up with due dates! When you've gone through all the work and are ready to hand it in, do it with a good attitude so I'll think you've put your best work into it. Not: "Here's this stupid paper you wanted." That makes me feel as if you didn't do much work on it—as if you don't value it.)

- *If you don't want to do it over, do it right the first time!* (Pay attention to the rubric on the assignment! Check your work over before you hand it in. I don't like to be the bearer of bad news!)

- *If it's a school rule, follow it!* (If the handbook says, "No gum at school," don't ask me if you can chew gum. I follow rules.)

- *If you are supposed to have it, be sure you do, every day!* (Would you pay a carpenter who didn't bring his or her tools every day? A doctor? A mechanic? Get in the habit, it's a good one.)

- *If allowed time to work, use it wisely!* (If we have some extra time, I will be willing to let you work, not talk.)

- *If you gripe about the assignment, be prepared to do extra.* (I have carefully planned the work and activities we do in class. If I ask for a two-page paper that describes the setting and main characters in a book we've read, I don't

---

In Search of Effective Discipline

If you are interested in designing a set of strategies to control student behavior in your school, we suggest you take the following steps.

1. **Develop a site team.**
   A few heads are better than one.

2. **Be creative.**
   Incorporate into your plan those problem-solving strategies you teach your students to use.

3. **Be flexible.**
   Try it; you might like it!

4. **Communicate with colleagues.**
   Realize we all have different areas of strength. Use them.

5. **Read for management ideas.**
   Read everything: education journals, women's magazines, even *Popular Science!*

6. **Keep parents involved.**
   They are eager to be on the team.

7. **Share your successes.**
   You'll soon enjoy hearing about them from the community!

8. **Most of all, love the kids!**

want to hear, "Golly, two pages. Do we *have* to write two pages? What if we...." It's not "Let's Make a Deal" here. I'll just say, "Gee, I think you can write three or four pages on yours.")

- *If you are angry, bite the bullet!* (Sometimes something happens in another class or between classes that can really make you upset. Come to me before class, just let me know that you are upset, and I'll try to keep things safe for you. But, if someone looks at you, says "Hi," or smiles at someone else in the classroom, don't bite their head off and start WW III in my room!)

Standards To Dress By
In order to help with discipline, my advice to a first-year teacher is to look professional. Look like you are dressed for an important job. (Interestingly enough, I find that age is not a factor here, only grooming.)

If you look like you are ready to pick weeds or rake leaves, you'll probably have better luck doing that than teaching a classroom full of energized students. Jeans, sweat pants, sloppy-looking clothes make you look "at ease." Students interpret those vibes as "Sic 'em! They're ready to play!"

A high school teacher I know wears suits to school the first week—a jacket, scarf or tie, and skirt. During the second week, she leaves the suit jacket off as long as she has control in the classroom. If the students start getting loud, on goes the jacket. As the students practice good behavior, they learn that she will remain in charge.

Look important; feel important.

Sharon Wilson's Classroom Initiatives

I started teaching when my own kids were in high school, which I feel gives me a degree of insight into student behavior. My first year at Intermediate was basically noneventful except for my seventh grade developmental reading class, which was the last hour of the day.

Have you ever noticed that developmental students also have an inability to stay on task and will misbehave to keep someone from noticing that they are experiencing academic problems? Well, you can imagine trying to teach 20 students like this all together at the end of the day! Do you hear the theme to "Mission Impossible" playing?

I have found that the following techniques can help such students understand the importance of rules and develop independence and self-discipline.

Mastery Learning
In October, Vickie came to our faculty meeting and shared information

---

Many management problems can be avoided by providing two things: (1) clear guidelines for behavior and work procedures and (2) engaging instruction.

about requiring students to demonstrate mastery. Many teachers didn't think this would work, but I didn't question it. I was willing to try anything to get students to stay on task and out of trouble.

At the time, I was using a newspaper as my primary resource with my developmental students. In keeping with the mastery concept, I decided to check off each daily newspaper assignment, assess it according to pre-established outcomes, and require 85 percent mastery. The amount of time my developmental students spent on task increased dramatically!

Self-Monitoring Forms

Another component that I use from time to time is a self-monitoring form on which the students can monitor their own conduct by focusing on a specific behavior that needs improving, such as talking without permission. We would do this daily, keep it on file, and from time to time, I would assess the results individually with students.

Color-Coded Cards

After Jana shared the classroom rules with the other teachers, Vickie helped me establish a color-coded card system to be used with the rules. I wrote each rule on a poster board in a different color. I then put that corresponding color on an index-card. Now, if after one verbal warning, a student breaks a rule, I simply lay a card on his or her desk. The student signs, dates, and hands the card back to me. I keep the cards filed by class in a file box on my desk. When a student collects three of any color, I assign detention.

This has proved to be a great success, and instruction time is not interrupted by "What did I do?" The student knows the exact rule he or she has broken by looking at the color on the displayed chart. I might add that rarely are students "surprised" when I assign detention. After all, they have received clear warnings. The card method also enables me to nip problems in the bud. With this system, behavior problems are handled before they reach the out-of-control state.

Traffic-Control Cards

When students appear to need a more structured environment in which to perform independent tasks (in other words, a way to regulate classroom traffic), I use a self-checking index-card strategy.

First, I place index cards numbered in order from one through 10 inside library-book pockets attached to the wall by the entry door. If a student wants to help correct papers or complete a special learning activity at our learning table, he or she takes the next available card. After class instruction, whoever has cards one through three will go to complete their independent tasks. Whenever a card is returned to its pocket, the student with the next number goes to the table.

Rita Cavin's Classroom Initiatives

I have come to realize that many management problems can be avoided by providing two things: (1) clear guidelines for behavior and work procedures and (2) engaging instruction.

Clear Guidelines

I'm not sure why this obvious fact escaped me for such a long time. But as a school teacher, I made many assumptions about students' behavior and work habits. I assumed they knew what was expected of them and that they knew the processes they needed to follow to meet those expectations. As my colleagues and I examined these assumptions, we realized that students and staff desperately needed a common culture that established the criteria for work and behavior. We learned never to take standards for granted. Before we ask students for anything now, we make our guidelines clear to everyone involved.

Engaging Instruction

In reading about effective practice in middle schools, staff members found many references to cooperative learning—how it actively engaged learners and seemed to minimize behavior problems. We found that Johnson and Johnson's book *Circles of Learning*, was a valuable guide. Several of our faculty spent time reading professional literature on the subject and passing new information on to the rest of the staff. As many have before us, we compiled an impressive array of techniques for structuring classes for cooperative learning.

However, I would often try what seemed like a well-organized and prepared lesson only to hit major snags. It seemed that my students were not as well trained in cooperative learning as I'd assumed they were. That was discouraging. It meant backtracking and re-planning and re-doing. For many teachers around me, it meant they had an excuse for abandoning cooperative learning altogether and doing what they'd always done.

Because I teach social studies and geography, I felt compelled to keep searching for ways to get my students to cooperate with one another. It just seemed to be the democratic thing to do. And it seemed like a motivating way to learn. After more reading and support from our principal, we discovered that the key to successful cooperative groups lies totally in the groundwork. (That brings me back to my first point about the need to provide students with clear expectations and work guidelines.)

We began to teach the students the general process involved in cooperative learning. This is often called *group process* and fundamentally means that all the general rules, reasons, purposes, and procedures of group work are dealt with before any assignments are made. We found that the first two weeks of each new school year were an excellent time for teaching process. During that time, each

> *We realized that students and staff desperately needed a common culture that established the criteria for work and behavior.*

teacher in a team would teach a different segment of the process. This way, all the students were involved in all the aspects of process without having to hear it six or seven times. After establishing the guidelines and signal words or cues, each teacher in a team would have all students familiar with all the necessary background.

We found that having common rules and cues in our team simplifies life for everyone involved. Because our sixth graders come from self-contained classrooms, usually with a single teacher, into our teams of five core teachers, unifying the team helps both students and parents with the adjustment.

One special part of the general group process we teach our students is a technique for listening. In 1991, our school counselor arranged for a special assembly from Motivational Media Assemblies, Inc., of Burbank, California. As part of the program, the presenters furnished students with materials to help them develop interpersonal skills. In these materials, we discovered and adopted as our school's own, a listening technique called OLE (we pronounce it *oh-lay*). Students are taught three steps to effective listening:

1. Open posture; uncross legs and arms.
2. Lean forward.
3. Make eye contact.

This has proved to be effective in the classroom and in larger groups of students in helping students to focus their attention.

Looking back, it seems more than obvious that we all do better when we know what is expected of us. This applies to adults and students alike. My job as the "teacher" is to equip each student with tools they can use to build their own learning. Teaching process helps me do that job.

Conclusion

"We are having a great day at Chickasha Intermediate" is the slogan we use when we answer the telephone at school these days, and this is totally appropriate. It reflects the school that Intermediate has become.

We have happy kids and parents. Student attendance is up, and when we have student-led parent conferences at the end of the first and third nine weeks, 97 percent of parents attend. During open house, our auditorium is standing room only.

We've come a long way from the days when large numbers of students acted out, when many staff members withdrew, and when many parents fretted. Today, we are a team that is meeting its mission—Success for All, Now and Tomorrow.

Today, we are a school that operates on two key words: pride and respect.

Innovative Discipline Reproducible 1.1

The OLE Listening Technique

We teach our students three steps to effective listening:

1. Open posture; uncross legs and arms.

2. Lean forward.

3. Make eye contact.

This technique has proved to be effective in the classroom and in larger groups in helping students focus their attention.

*Innovative Discipline
Reproducible 1.2a*

Before You Implement Cooperative Learning

The following guidelines can help minimize any problems that might occur when you introduce cooperative learning procedures.

1. **Start slowly.**
   Use cooperative learning sparingly until you are sure that what you are doing is benefiting your class.

2. **Avoid group grading.**
   Group grading can alarm parents of high achievers. Group grading is only for skilled practitioners of cooperative learning, and then only when adequate parent and administrator information has been provided in advance.

3. **Build an atmosphere that encourages cooperative learning.**
   Building student ownership, active participation, high expectations, and positive feelings creates a foundation for cooperative learning and for successful classroom management.

4. **Promote student success.**
   Early experiences with cooperative learning should be highly successful and rewarding for students.

5. **Tell administrators you are using cooperative learning methods.**
   Be ready to explain your goals, expected outcomes, and the benefits that research associates with cooperative learning.

Innovative Discipline Reproducible 1.2b

Before You Implement Cooperative Learning
(Continued)

6. **Use other techniques and strategies as well as cooperative learning.**
   No technique is effective when used all the time.

7. **Monitor student reactions and conduct individual conferences with students.**
   This helps reassure those who are troubled by cooperative learning.

8. **Teach group process to students.**
   Don't expect your students to already have the skills needed to work successfully in groups.

9. **Monitor the effectiveness of your teaching.**
   Use the same individual evaluation procedures you usually use. You may also wish to monitor student achievement; attitude; attendance; discipline referrals; and behavior in the playground, hallway, and lunchroom as indicators of the success of your methods.

10. **Network with other teachers.**
    A support group of other teachers who use cooperative learning is necessary for problem solving, celebration, and exchange of ideas.

SOURCE: *Cooperative Learning in the Elementary Classroom*, by Lawrence Lyman, Harvey C. Foyle, and Tara S. Azwell. Washington, D. C.: National Education Association, 1993.

Reader Reflections

Insights: _____
_____
_____
_____
_____
_____

Actions for Our School (District) To Consider: _____
_____
_____
_____
_____
_____
_____
_____

Teacher Review

Building Parent Partnerships
ENGAGING HARD-TO-REACH PARENTS

The article, "Engaging Hard-to-Reach Parents," is very insightful because building parent partnerships is one of the biggest problems I face as a teacher. It sometimes seems like a struggle for me to get parents to take responsibility for the actions of their children. Nonetheless, establishing open communication is necessary in order to create a productive learning environment, and interacting with parents helps me to understand how important they are to the learning process.

The suggestions provided in this story are useful in encouraging parental involvement and building a trusting relationship between parents and school personnel. For instance, I agree with the idea that schools should make transportation available to parents who cannot get to school-related events on their own. Also, childcare is very difficult and expensive for single-parent households, so providing before-and after-school programs is a great way to show parents that their involvement at school is important. Additionally, I like the idea of establishing a Parent Executive Council that would relate parental concerns to school administration.

Parents have more power to cause change than the teacher does. They help to reinforce concepts that we are teaching inside the classroom, and they help us understand their child's learning style. We need to provide opportunities for parents to see themselves as an important part of their child's education. Some parents are ashamed of their own educational inadequacies and avoid contact with school personnel. We must keep the lines of communication open and build trust. Not only will this enable parents to support the learning process at home, but the message will reach the community that the students are learning and happy and that the teachers care. Parents are resources that must be used wisely!

Simone Matlock-Phillips
Middle School Teacher
Chestnut Accelerated Middle School
Springfield, Massachusetts

ENGAGING HARD-TO-REACH PARENTS

Fed up with parents' excuses, these teachers found a way to identify and remove the barriers to parent involvement.

2

If you could dream of the "perfect school or the perfect school day," what would it be? Would you include an active parental involvement program? Would that program be based on parental support or parental demands? At Teachers Memorial School, we have a very active parent involvement program based on a philosophy of parental support and trust rather than on parental demands.

Our parent program is driven by the passion to do what is best for each student. This is a program that is not easy to develop and is difficult to maintain. It is, nonetheless, one of the most rewarding and gratifying programs at Teachers Memorial School, located in Kinston, North Carolina. Our school serves approximately 360 children in grades K-2, as well as a Head Start program.

Teachers Memorial

THERESA ABERNETHY and LAURA LAVIN
Teachers Memorial School
Kinston, North Carolina

School is part of the Lenoir County Public School System. Lenoir County is approximately 100 miles east of the capital of Raleigh and 100 miles west of the coast. The county's financial base is primarily agricultural, although many industries, such as Dupont, White-Westinghouse, and Lenox, do business in the area.

The community surrounding Teachers Memorial School is predominantly black and the poverty level is very high. Seventy percent of our students receive public assistance through Aid to Families with Dependent Children, free and reduced price breakfast and lunch programs, federal public housing, as well as other state and federally funded welfare programs. More than 60 percent of our students' parents did not complete high school. Seventy percent of our students' households are headed by a single parent. Fifty percent of our students' parents are unemployed.

Parent Mistrust Of Schools

Before we began our parent involvement program, we had a real problem getting parents to participate in their child's education. Many parents had a lack of enthusiasm for our programs because of past negative experiences with the education system.

Our challenge was to work successfully with these parents in the best interests of their children, and to increase their involvement by building trust.

Teachers and other staff members at Teachers Memorial School readily accepted this challenge.

Our goals were to get parents to come and volunteer in our classrooms, to increase attendance at Parents' Night meetings, and to get parent support for our discipline plan. Teachers at our school realized that if we wanted parents to feel comfortable in our classrooms, we had to reach out to them in ways that would make them trust the teachers. Because many parents have had negative school experiences, it was difficult and even painful for some of them to visit a school.

Our efforts have resulted in increased parent participation in school programs and greater ties between school and the community. Teachers Memorial has also been presented with two very exciting awards: North Carolina's first Entrepreneurial Award and the Best of State Award from Redbook Magazine.

Training Staff to Collaborate

Before we could build trust among parents, we realized we needed to build teamwork and collaboration among school staff. We received help doing this from the Consortium for the Advancement of Public Education (C.A.P.E.). C.A.P.E. is a network of educators in eastern North Carolina that provides training in teamwork and consensus building. With the assistance of C.A.P.E., our faculty began to realize our dream of making Teachers Memorial School a school where "Everybody is Somebody Special."

We began with a staff retreat to the Coastline Inn in Wilmington, North Carolina. There, our staff began learning about the concepts of cooperation and collaboration. These retreats have become annual events and have allowed us time to build an understanding of our own needs and the importance of working together to encourage change.

Searching for Grants and Resources

Along with our staff retreats, we sought help from the Comer School Project, a school reform initiative based at Yale

Seventy percent of our students receive public assistance through Aid to Families with Dependent Children.

University. The Comer Project was founded on the principles of parental involvement, site-based decision making, and participatory leadership. We used funds made available from the Comer Project and Chapter I to increase parental involvement at Teachers Memorial. Those funds made it possible for us to stage family night dinners and other events where faculty, students, and parents could become acquainted in a non-threatening environment.

Building Parent Trust

Family Night Dinners

The first part of our plan was to make parents feel welcome in our school. We held special training sessions that taught parents some simple and helpful techniques for working more successfully with their children. Staff members selected topics such as homework and building academic skills. Then staff took turns presenting information on math and reading activities to the parents.

We provided dinner and child care for parents that attended the meetings. These dinners helped set the stage for developing trust between parents and teachers. The dinners provided an informal session for parents and teachers to talk to each other.

Parents Executive Council

After we began to build trust between parents and staff through our informal dinners, we encouraged parents to get involved with the decision-making process at Teachers Memorial School. We asked parents to become active members of our Parents Executive Council. This group has about 14 active members. Parents can remain on the council as long as their children are enrolled at Teachers Memorial School. The Parents Executive Council provides guidance and direction to Teachers Memorial, offers community-based action programs, and assists the principal with community relations.

As a member of the Parents Executive Council since its conception, Ms. Darvetta Bryant offers a perspective on how the body assists the school. "We call or go to the homes of some of our hard-to-reach parents. We offer to help that parent with the child or help the parent get to school for conferences with the teacher. Several times we are called upon to make sure our parents know about activities."

Parent-Teacher Retreat

During the third year of our site-based decision-

> **Tips for Building Parent Trust**
>
> To encourage parental involvement, a relationship of trust must be built between parents and school staff. Here are some ways we sought to build that trust:
>
> - Create effective communication systems so parents know what's going on at your school. Develop a newsletter or create a school hotline.
> - Be willing to participate in the same activities you ask parents to become a part of.
> - Include parents in all planning activities for the school. The more parents that are involved, the easier it is to accomplish your goals.
> - Strive to eliminate barriers to parental involvement, such as a lack of child care and lack of transportation.
> - Break goals down into manageable tasks whose success can be easily measured.

making program, we invited the Parents Executive Council to attend our faculty's annual planning retreat. The ideas expressed during the retreat propelled us into new avenues of action. For example, the parents council created a survey of parents on their perception of the school. The survey asked parents whether staff effectively addressed the needs of students and their families. The council also created a survey to gain demographic information about families at our school. These parent surveys have given us a better understanding of parents and their needs. We have used this information to decide future activities, apply for grants, and study where to go next. Overall, the retreat proved to be a tremendous foundation for trust and relationship-building between parents and teachers.

Meeting Parents' Basic Needs

Telephone Hotline and Saturday Hours

Not all parents are able to appear at Parents' Night meetings or other weekday activities. To meet the needs of those parents, we sent weekly and monthly newsletters to notify parents of any upcoming events. We created a "Telephone Hotline" to allow parents to call the school at any time to get their child's homework assignments, cafeteria menus, and a calendar of special events. Parents are also encouraged to use the hotline to leave a message for the principal or a teacher. And, telephones were installed in our classrooms, enabling teachers to call parents whenever necessary. Our principal initiated a "Saturday Hours Program" to make himself more available to parents who are unable to visit school during the week.

Child Care and Transportation

Many of our students come from single-parent homes and finding child care is difficult and expensive. We sought a way of easing parents' burden of caring for their "latch key" children. We began a program that allows parents to drop off their children as early as 6:30 a.m. and pick them up by 6:00 p.m. The startup funds for this program came from a grant. The ongoing expenses for the program are paid for by the parents of the children in the program.

We also bought a bus to help parents get to school for parent night dinners, parent-teacher conferences, and other school events. We send the buses out to pick up parents who don't have cars. Our willingness to help parents solve a basic need such as transportation, shows them how important we deem their involvement in school activities.

Many parents had a lack of enthusiasm for our programs because of past negative experiences with the education system.

Building Trust On Parents' Turf

Our dinners, retreats, and after-school programs were great ways to make parents feel more comfortable visiting Teachers Memorial School. We realized, however, that we could gain more parent trust and support by going into the community where they lived.

Community Parties

A few years ago we started Family Night where we invited parents to come out for a night of hot dogs. We offered free food, along with free soft drinks and musical entertainment. Anyone related to a child at our school—parents, grandparents, aunts, and uncles—were free to come. We didn't make any "pitches" for parent involvement at these events. It was just a time to have fun and mingle.

Family Night has grown in the past few years to include the neighborhood as well as parents and teachers. It has become a big block party sponsored by the school. This has gone a long way to help parents see our school as a friendly place where they can feel comfortable.

Project "Read Out"

Another way we reached out to the surrounding community was through "Project Read Out," a satellite reading and parental involvement program. We held the program at community centers in the four public housing projects where a majority of our students live. The program was offered each Saturday for two hours.

We received a grant from Chapter I to provide the funds for hiring a coordinator, two assistants, and parent contacts at each of the community centers in the housing projects.

We purchased many books with familiar stories for this program. The children came with their parents to the centers and listened as staff members read stories. These staff members modeled correct methods of reading stories to the children, and proper ways of assessing children's understanding of the stories. Children were allowed to check out books to be read at home. Many of our children participated with their entire families. Some of the children that were in our first

How to Handle Hard-to-Reach Parents

You've probably heard every excuse in the book by now when it comes to getting parents involved. Here are some ways to get through to parents who resist participation in school activities.

- Provide child care during Parent Night dinners and conferences. Don't give parents an excuse not to appear.
- Provide transportation to school functions for those who need it.
- Make parent get-togethers lively and fun by offering door prizes, refreshments, and other incentives. Be creative.
- Reward parents for their involvement. Offer coupons to restaurants, for example.
- Go out into the community and meet the parents on their own turf. Many feel less intimidated by teachers in their own homes.
- Make phone calls and send notes to hard-to-reach parents reminding them of scheduled conferences.
- Create a newsletter written by parents for parents.

Project Read Out program are entering kindergarten this year. These children and their parents feel better about entering school for the first time because they are now familiar with some of the staff.

Bartering with Business for Resources

The staff of Teachers Memorial is always searching for ways to reach out to local businesses and community agencies in our efforts to help parents.

We've formed something of a barter system with Head Start, the County Parks and Recreation Department, the Boys and Girls Club, hospitals, and other local businesses. These are mutually beneficial arrangements for the school and the community agency.

Deals with Community Agencies

For example, our local Boys and Girls Club operates a satellite program at Teachers Memorial after school and during the summer. The Club provides tutors to help our students with their homework. They also make contributions to our school's capital improvements program and donate playground equipment. In turn, we allow the Boys and Girls Club to have use of a classroom during the afternoons.

We have a similar arrangement with Head Start. Head Start gets the space and school services it needs, including free lunch and breakfast. The head start students become familiar with the notion of school and kindergarten. In return for use of our school, Head Start built a fenced-in playground that all the students at Teachers Memorial can use.

We also joined forces with the County Parks and Recreation Department to build a community gym on school grounds. We gave them space on our school grounds and the department built the gym. We use the gym during the day for physical education classes and programs at school. The department, in turn, gets to use the gym as a recreation center at night.

Business Partnerships

Teachers Memorial was paired with Lenoir Memorial Hospital through the local school system's Adopt-A-School Program. It was a match made in heaven for our children, their families, and the hospital staff. The staff of Lenoir Memorial Hospital has provided workshops for our staff and students on a variety of medical topics. They have rewarded students who are "Good Citizens" of the month, with an end-of-year party. But perhaps the most significant way the hospital staff has helped our students is by providing Christmas gifts to the families of

We encouraged parents to get involved with the decision-making process at Teachers Memorial School.

many of our neediest students. This show of generosity has touched the entire Teachers Memorial community. In return, Teachers Memorial has provided book cases, crayons, coloring books, and other items to the hospital's pediatric unit for sick children.

Our partnership with the Dupont Kinston plant has also proven to be very successful. Dupont Plant personnel have supported Teachers Memorial by providing workshops for teachers, students, and their parents. Dupont Kinston has also helped train teachers on new computer technology and software applications. And, the company has donated computers, funding for special events, supplies, technological expertise, and video production facilities.

Parents as True Partners

Our successes in generating greater parental participation at Teachers Memorial School thus far are measurable. We've managed to eliminate some of the barriers to parent involvement by providing child care and transportation. We worked hard to help parents see our school as a friendly place that can help them meet their needs.

We are seeing greater involvement by our parents as evidenced by increasing attendance at Parent Dinners, greater numbers of visitors to our Saturday hours conferences, more participation in the Parents Executive Council, and many, many calls to our Hotline.

This increased participation reflects the success of our efforts to build a relationship of trust and comfort between school staff, parents, and the community. Our parents have become more comfortable with their children's learning environment. This comfort is reflected in the smiles on our students' faces, and in their eagerness to participate in the learning process. And the morale of our teachers is, of course, heightened by this greater participation, leading to better and better classroom performance.

Our challenge is to continue to realize our dreams for Teachers Memorial School. There are times when we become complacent with the success of our programs; we take them for granted both as parents and as faculty. The effort it takes to maintain our programs and draw greater parent participation is time- and labor-intensive. Finding additional sources of revenue for our programs is often an obstacle. We are unable to continue our Project Read Out program due to the loss of Title I funds. The funds were cut because of the change in formula in our local system.

Despite these obstacles, we haven't thrown up our hands and quit. We continue to seek funding. We've come too far and there is too much potential gain to allow a lack of funding to defeat us.

We have been able to make great strides in turning non-supportive parents into actively involved parents. We believe these parents will now set the standard for generations to come.

Building Parent Partnerships Reproducible 2.1

Want To Hook Hard-to-Reach-Parents?

Sometimes you need a gimmick or a hook to get hard-to-reach parents involved in school activities. Here are a few things you might try:

- Select a "Parent of the Week." That parent should come to school during his or her designated week. This gives parents a feeling of prestige.

- Sponsor a "Mother's Day Tea." Provide lunch and have students create and read poems or songs.

- Create "Father's Special Day" on Valentine's Day. Invite fathers to school for lunch.

- Hold a "Bring an Adult Day" where students can invite parents or other family members into the classroom for the day.

- Have a "Parent Talent Program" during the school year. Give parents an opportunity to show off their talents.

- Create parent-student role reversal exercises.

Building Parent Partnerships
Reproducible 2.2

School Hotlines

More and more schools are creating telephone hotlines to give busy parents access to information on school activities. Teachers Memorial School runs a 24-hour hotline for parents and the community. Parents can access the hotline using a touch-tone phone. Effective hotlines can include the following information:

- General instructions and menu of options

- Cafeteria menus and prices

- Calendar of weekly school events

- Study Helpers—Tips on How to Help Your Child Study

- Parent Conferences—Upcoming Schedule

- School Hours and Emergency Phone Numbers

THE ULTIMATE BEGINNER'S GUIDE

Building Parent Partnerships
Reproducible 2.3

Parent Survey

This survey will tell us how the school is doing in your eyes. Please do not write your name or your child's name anywhere on the form. To complete the form, read the question and make a mark in the column that best answers the question. Please be honest. If we are not doing the job you expect, we need to know. If we are doing well, we need to know that too. Please feel free to make any comments.

	Strongly Agree	Agree	Unsure	Disagree	Strongly Disagree
1. Do you think proper knowledge and training are provided to your child at _____ (school name)?					
2. Do you think the after school care program is beneficial?					
3. Is the playground safe and adequate for your child?					
4. Are you satisfied with your child's teacher?					
5. How important are the health services provided by the school to you?					
6. Are you satisfied with the principal at the school?					
7. Would you like to see the school hours changed?					
8. Do you think that parents should be more involved with their child's education?					
9. Do you think your child has too much homework?					
10. Are you satisfied with _____ (school name)?					
11. Does the staff at _____ (school name) make you feel welcome when you come to visit?					

Comments _____
_____

Building Parent Partnerships
Reproducible 2.4

Parent Information Survey

The purpose of this survey is to provide information concerning the demographics of our school so we can design programs to better meet the needs of our community. Won't you please take a moment and complete it? Thanks for your help. Please check the appropriate box. When a number is requested, write it in the box.

Are you a single parent?	Yes	No
How many children live in your household?	Number	
Do you own a television set?	Yes	No
Do you own a V.C.R.?	Yes	No
Do you own a car?	Yes	No
Do you own your home or do you rent?	Rent	Own
Are you the child's natural parent?	Yes	No
Have you moved in the last six months?	Yes	No
Do you have a phone?	Yes	No
Are you employed?	Yes	No
How many children do you have that will be attending _____ (school name) in the future?	Number	

Please help us help your child by completing this form.
Do not write your name or your child's name anywhere on this form.
Thank you.

THE ULTIMATE BEGINNER'S GUIDE

Reader Reflections

Insights: _____

_____

_____

_____

_____

_____

Actions for Our School (District) to Consider: _____

_____

_____

_____

_____

_____

_____

*If we want parents to feel
comfortable in our classrooms,
we have to reach out to them in ways
that make them trust teachers.*

Teacher Review

Integrated Thematic Teaching
CREATING CRITICAL THINKERS

It's a wonderful moment when hopeful candidates discover they will be teachers in the coming year. That moment, however, is quickly followed by fear when they recognize that there is a huge expanse of nothing where solid lesson plans should be. Developing entire classes from scratch is difficult, but Eileen Moreno's account, "Creating Critical Thinkers," is an excellent step-by-step guide to constructing meaningful curriculum for any teacher at any level.

Moreno makes a persuasive case for thematic teaching, as opposed to divorcing the subjects. We spend too much time separating and isolating in our schools, when, in reality, everything is connected. History, science, math, literature, art, and philosophy all continue to influence each other as they have done throughout human history. It's foolish to treat these subjects as unrelated elements that are dangerous when mixed together.

I'm a high school English teacher, and in my first year I found students resistant to the idea of studying history, philosophy, and art in an English class. I didn't have Moreno's model to work from or her eloquent explanation of why it's important to show students the links between these fundamentals. Moreno really believes in taking the time to explain to the students your goals in thematic teaching. She believes in making the children responsible for developing the themes and taking ownership of their instruction. That was the key I was missing in my own approach. I assumed students were ready to marry the subjects, not realizing I had to ask for their help in doing that job. I strongly urge new teachers to consider adapting Moreno's ideas in order to create a thematically connected curriculum that fosters critical thinking and meaningful, relevant lessons.

Jeff Shaw
English Teacher
Wells High School
Wells, Maine

CREATING CRITICAL THINKERS

In San Diego, a thematic unit on "change" turned a class of third graders into critical thinkers.

3

San Diego refers to itself as "America's finest city." Indeed, this is one of the reasons I chose to attend college here at the University of California, San Diego. Having visited San Diego often as a child, I knew that there was no other place where I'd rather study. By my senior year of college I had decided to become a teacher. I began by working as an aide at the middle and high school levels. When I went to work at an elementary school, however, I knew that was where I belonged.

I am currently a third grade bilingual GATE (Gifted and Talented Education) teacher at Emerson/Bandini Elementary in the San Diego Unified School district. We are located in a tough part of town with its share of problems. It is a low-income neighborhood with a population that is primarily African-American and Latino. Despite the hardships of being located in an economically disadvantaged area, Emerson/Bandini is always on the cutting edge of education. In 1995, we were recognized nationally with the 1995 Achieving School Award by the Title I Academic Excellence Program.

Making education richer and more meaningful is not an easy task. The days of teaching straight from the teacher's guide and using worksheets are long gone. We constantly hear about the need to challenge our students, to encourage higher level thinking skills, and to make learning a worthwhile experience for the kids. At this point you may say, "Sounds great, but how can I create such a learning environment in my classroom?" The answer lies in thematic instruction.

In recent years, there has been a growing trend

EILEEN MORENO
Bilingual Gifted and Talented Education Teacher
Grade 3
Emerson/Bandini Elementary School
San Diego, California

THE ULTIMATE BEGINNER'S GUIDE

toward thematic instruction. In my quest to learn more about this strategy, I realized that there was much more to it than my colleagues and I thought. I questioned the experts, I read from the experts, and soon I felt like an expert. Once I had developed and implemented my thematic units, I was ready to pass on what I knew about the outcomes of thematic instruction to my colleagues in a more formal forum. I had the opportunity to do so at a teacher-to-teacher conference in our district. I was pleased to help clarify questions other teachers had about thematic units. I had many questions and frustrations myself when I started my journey into the world of themes. It was, and continues to be, an exciting and ever-changing experience.

Why Integrated Thematic Instruction?

Integrated thematic instruction is a strategy which helps to unify the disciplines in a richer and more meaningful manner, while promoting the critical thinking skills we want our students to develop. It is a practical method of teaching. Thematic instruction allows you to devote more time to a specific concept in which you and your students may be particularly interested, rather than jumping around from one chapter to the next without unification of ideas or concepts. With thematic instruction I am able to connect different topics within the subject areas. This gives students an opportunity to learn certain topics and concepts in depth.

Although the thematic approach was adopted by the San Diego Unified Gifted and Talented Education Department, it is not a strategy that should be limited to gifted students only. Thematic interdisciplinary curriculum currently is advocated by the California State Frameworks as an important curriculum component for all students.

Integrated Thematic Unit

The first thing that you must decide in planning your unit is the theme. A theme is a universal concept that should help to integrate various topics of study. Integrating subjects allows students to make connections between the subject areas. This in turn promotes more complex and meaningful understandings about the theme. Themes are meant to be open-ended or universal. This allows many topics to be incorporated and integrated within a theme. For example, think about the theme "relationships." This is a huge concept that can include just about all of the subject areas that we teach. In any

Thematic instruction allows you to devote time to a specific concept, rather than jumping around from one chapter to the next.

good novel there are always relationships to explore. Science and math are made up of ever-changing relationships, and of course, social studies consists of the relationships between people and societies. You can see there is a purpose for having universal concepts or themes that will allow you to truly unify all of your topic areas. And as I mentioned earlier, universal themes allow room for thought-provoking discussions that engage students in critical thinking and problem solving. Here's how I used a unit on "Change" to turn my third graders into critical thinkers.

Thematic Units And Curriculum Requirements

Most of us do not work at schools where thematic teaching has been formally adopted. There are usually many subject areas and special programs we have to teach. Thematic instruction doesn't have to interfere with anything else that you must teach, and it shouldn't feel like a burden. What it should—and will do—is enhance the quality of learning.

It is important to keep your district's curriculum requirements in mind when planning a thematic unit. In my district, for example, the fifth grade social studies curriculum is United States History. Therefore, a fifth grade teacher can't very well decide to teach a thematic unit on Greek history instead.

It is possible, however, to teach thematic units and satisfy your district's curriculum requirements. That is exactly what I did.

In choosing a theme for my class, I found it best to start by looking at all of the topics I had to cover in social studies. The first unit in my third grade social studies text consists of three chapters on the regions (mountains, lakes, rivers, plains, and deserts). I decided that "Change" would be an excellent theme into which the regions could be easily included. In addition, I quickly came to the conclusion that change occurs in every aspect of life so I knew that I wouldn't have a problem with this theme in any of my other subject areas, including language arts, science, and math.

Components of a Thematic Unit

Now that I knew what my theme would be it was time to come up with

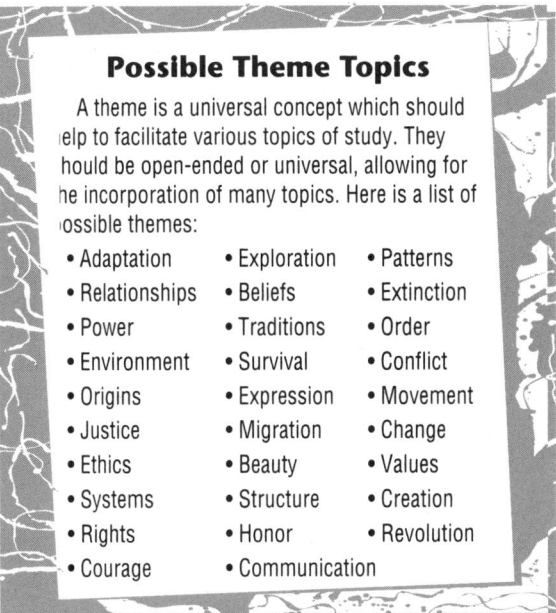

Possible Theme Topics

A theme is a universal concept which should help to facilitate various topics of study. They should be open-ended or universal, allowing for the incorporation of many topics. Here is a list of possible themes:

- Adaptation
- Relationships
- Power
- Environment
- Origins
- Justice
- Ethics
- Systems
- Rights
- Courage
- Exploration
- Beliefs
- Traditions
- Survival
- Expression
- Migration
- Beauty
- Structure
- Honor
- Communication
- Patterns
- Extinction
- Order
- Conflict
- Movement
- Change
- Values
- Creation
- Revolution

some generalizations about "Change."

Generalizations— The Key to Critical Thinking

A generalization expands on the meaning of the theme. It promotes critical and creative thinking, problem solving, logic, and interpretation. For example, in my unit on "Change," I chose the following four generalizations:

1. Change can be posi-

tive or negative
  2. Change is irreversible
  3. Change can be natural or man made
  4. One change causes another

I then challenge my students to examine the reliability and validity of each generalization. Naturally, generalizations are not necessarily valid all of the time. Thus, students engage in interesting dis-

It is possible to teach thematic units and satisfy your district's curriculum requirements.

course while challenging each other's opinions.

The generalizations force students to think creatively and solve problems.

Introducing Your Theme and Generalizations

I display my theme and generalizations prominently in my classroom. I found it a good idea to make banners that contain the generalizations. Once my room environment is set up, I introduce the theme and generalizations to my students. I began the "Change" theme by having the kids tell me anything that came to mind when they heard the word "change." We had a brainstorming session and I wrote down everything the students said. The following is the list that my students generated when asked "Where Does Change Occur?"

Clothes, time, school, home, friends, adaptation, laws, feelings, weather, seasons, months, growing, grades, point of view, furniture, presidents, nature, projects, traditions, classroom life, body, moving day, (light to dark)

I intend to do three things in creating the list. First, I want to get students thinking about change and see how much they already know. Second, I want to empower students to have some control over their learning. They feel empowered since they are being taught about things that they generated and that they have interest in. Finally, the list is a great source to refer to once I'm ready to introduce the generalizations.

I conduct a full lesson on each of the generalizations included in the theme. It is important to devote ample attention to each generalization, since students will continually refer back to them throughout the unit.

Here's an example of a lesson I taught around the generalization that "Change is irreversible."

I placed students in small groups to discuss how change is irreversible. The student wrote down as many examples of this as possible. This generalization proved to be a bit tricky because the students soon figured out that in many cases change is reversible. Thus, they found out right away that the generalizations are not to be taken as facts all of the time. This is something that I did not have to tell them. They figured it out themselves, discussed the inconsistencies, and decided to make two separate lists—one for reversible and another for irreversible changes.

Students' examples of change included the following statements.
- If you pull out the roots of a plant it won't grow again.
- If you cut your hair it will grow back.
- If you become paralyzed you cannot walk again.
- If your tire goes flat you can put air in it again.
- When an adult loses a tooth, it won't grow back again.
- If a car crashes or breaks down it can be fixed again.

I went through the same process of group brainstorming for each of the generalizations. At the end of each lesson, the students shared their responses with the class and their group work was put up on the theme bulletin board.

Integrating Academic Subjects Into Your Theme

Here's how I use the four generalizations to show students connections between the theme and their academic subjects including language arts, math, science, and social studies.

Language Arts

As part of a language arts lesson, I had students read a book called *The Little House*. This was the story of a little house that was built out in the country. Over a period of many years a huge city was built around the house. Nobody wanted to live in the little house. The house became run down and miserable because it missed the country. There were a myriad of changes that occurred throughout the story. I had students make a list of all of the changes present in the story. I always like to start out by making lists related to the theme so that the students can refer to them later. Next, I had students study the relationship between the four generalizations and the story. The most interesting lesson I had with my students was in studying the generalization, "Change can be positive or negative." I presented the following question, "Is changing the country into a city positive or negative?" It was obvious that there was not going to be consensus right away. I then decided to have a very simple debate. The students got into two groups, those who felt that changing the country into a city was positive versus those who felt it was negative. Then we went back and forth with each group giving reasons for their stance. Some of the reasons they generated included the following:
- More schools in city/ Not enough space to play in city
- More people = more friends/Too noisy in city
- More stores in city/ Too much contamination in city
- More places to go in city/Can't see the stars in city
- Better T.V. reception in city/More dangerous in city
- Easier access to emergency service in city/ Less nature in the city.

By the time students finished the debate a few of the kids had changed their minds and decided to move from one group to the other. The kids had a lot of fun, they learned a lot from each other and gained a better understanding and appreciation about the place where they live (city) or wish to live (countryside).

Best of all, it was a meaningful discussion that promoted critical thinking. And, the debate was controlled by the students rather than me.

The level of thinking my students achieved surpassed my expectations.

Social Studies
I found it easy to relate our chapters on regions and ecology to the theme of "Change."

The students understood that regions have changed dramatically over time. Through the use of the theme and generalizations, students were able to explore the consequences of regional changes that occurred in the past and continue to occur. Some of my students argued that the regional and ecological changes are all created by men who are greedy, that this change is negative, irreversible and will eventually destroy the planet.

On the other hand, some students argued that ecological changes occur naturally over time, that some regional changes are actually good for the environment and that these changes are not necessarily irreversible if they are handled responsibly.

Science
Science is a subject that fit naturally within the theme of "Change." Science is an ever-changing process, whether you study plants, health, animals, geology, biology, or chemistry.

In my unit we were studying health. We discussed the changes that occur in the body as we grow. We also discussed taking care of our body and the consequences of mistreating our body. If you look back on the four generalizations, I'm sure you will readily see how they can all relate to this topic. My students came to the conclusions that mistreating your body by smoking caused negative changes such as cancer and the consequences of these changes were irreversible. They found out that some changes in the body were natural but others were caused by man. For example, some people develop asthma due to the air pollution. This is a change in the body that is caused by man. On the other hand, there are many other changes within the body that are quite natural such as growing old.

Studying health issues within a theme framework proved to be much more eye opening and significant to students. They weren't just learning facts, they were thinking analytically, investigating, and applying these facts to their own lives.

Mathematics
For mathematics, my students studied statistics in relationship to population studies. They then examined the effects of changing factors such as death, birth, migration, and immigration on the outcome of their statistical analysis and interpretation.

After doing some very simple statistical experiments with changing factors, I asked my students to think about how these

▸ BEST OF TEACHER-TO-TEACHER

changes affect population studies. Then I guided them right back toward the generalizations again. Are mathematics affected by change? Are the consequences of changing factors in statistics positive or negative? Is it possible to manipulate the numbers so that change can be reversed? In statistics, does one changing factor cause another?

Common Questions

There are a few commonly asked questions about thematic instruction.

Q: "Do I have to relate every subject area into the theme?"

A: No. Generally we teach math, social studies, language arts, science, music, art and physical education. It is not always possible to include every single subject area into the theme. You do not want to stretch the relationship between the theme and the subject too much or you will simply confuse your students and they will lose interest. For example, if I chose the theme "Revolution," I would be hard pressed to find a way to relate this to physical education. On the other hand, some themes such as "Change" relate themselves very well to all of the subject areas. However, you should not feel pressured to include everything into your unit or be discouraged from teaching thematically because you can't include everything. Generally it works fine if you are able to include at least three of the subject areas into your theme.

Q: How often should I actually teach lessons related to the theme?

A: This is up to you. Obviously we all have a million and a half things to cover throughout the year and thematic instruction cannot take the place of everything. Thematic teaching does not have to occur around the clock in order to be effective. Formal lessons are given once you feel students have made connections between the theme and their studies. Usually you should find yourself able to give at least a couple of thematic lessons per week. However, you should not let weeks go by without having a thematic lesson or else it will become a meaningless activity for the students.

Q: How often should I change my themes?

A: Once again, this is up to you. You may decide to change your theme every quarter/semester or you may even decide to keep the same theme all year long if it appropriately relates to everything. Again, "Change" is a good example of a theme that can easily be kept for an entire year. If you are thinking that the children would get bored with the same theme all year long, think again. Remember that a theme is universal. It is not narrow and one-sided. Moreover, the topics surrounding the theme are constantly changing so that the students are always looking at the theme from different perspectives.

Changing Themes

Personally, I changed my theme every quarter (nine weeks). The first quarter I taught "Traditions." The second quarter I taught "Adaptation." For the third quarter and part of the fourth, I taught "Change."

Challenge to Students

If all of this seems to be very complicated, it is. But it is meant to be this way. Only complicated material will challenge our students and provoke critical thinking. And if the basics are taught well, then the relationship between the topics and the theme will jump out at the students. It may seem a bit hard to believe that third graders can have so much to offer. Yet I found my students had lots to say on the subject of "Change." I must confess that at times I was very surprised at what they had to say. However, upon reflecting on the objectives of thematic instruction, I see that these higher level thinking skills are a natural part of studying universal concepts and generalizations.

"A Ha!" Moments

Perhaps the most rewarding part of teaching thematically was when I realized that the kids were not only seeing the relationship between the subjects and the theme. They began to point out to me the relationship between the different themes themselves! For example, my students soon began seeing the relationship between the previously learned theme "Adaptation" and the current theme "Change." They began saying things like, "When the country changed into the city the little house had to adapt to living in the city," "When your body changes and you get very sick you have to adapt to going to the doctor a lot," and "If they keep chopping down trees, the air is going to change and we are going to have to adapt to dirty air." The first time my students referred back to previously learned themes I was amazed. Despite the success I'd had in teaching each theme separately, I hadn't considered that the students' level of thinking would go above and beyond into relating the themes to each other.

Student/Parent Feedback

Teaching thematically has been wonderful. The level of thinking that my students achieved surpassed my expectations. Despite the extra work involved, I have thoroughly enjoyed teaching thematically and more importantly I feel that my students have enjoyed it as well. In addition, the parental feedback was also positive. Here's an example of positive feedback generated by theme work. In low income areas it is not unusual to have high transiency rates. Many of our children transfer between two or more elementary schools. Needless to say, it is a big change for children and one that requires many adaptations. One of

You should not feel pressured to include everything into your unit, or be discouraged because you can't include everything.

my colleagues whose thematic units included "Adaptation," had a parent tell her that studying this theme had really made a difference for her child. Her little girl had come to realize that adaptation is a necessary part of life and one has to make the best of a situation.

After studying "Adaptation" in my own classroom I also noticed a greater amount of empathy among my students toward the new kids who arrived after the school year had begun.

Perhaps the best way to sum up my feelings of success is by giving you a quote from a student written in answer to the question, "What did you learn and how did you feel about the themes you studied?" She answered, "I really liked learning about traditions, adaptation and change. Now I know how important traditions are to the world and I want to continue my family traditions. I have a doll that my mom gave me and I think that I will take good care of it so I can give it to my daughter and she can do the same. I learned a lot about adaptation and how hard it can be to adapt to different things but I also know that if I don't adapt I probably won't be happy. I also learned that change happens all of the time but it affects everyone differently. I liked learning the themes because it was fun." ◆

Integrated Thematic Teaching
Reproducible 3.1

Ten Tips for Thematic Teaching

1. Pick your theme carefully
Be sure you don't forge ahead with a theme only to find out too late that it doesn't relate well to all of the topics you intend to teach.

2. Make your theme and generalizations very visible
Your theme and generalizations need to be evident to anyone who enters your classroom. Post banners prominently in your room.

3. Fill your classroom library with books that can be related to the theme
It is a good idea to make everything in your classroom as theme related as possible. Having a library filled with books that relate to the theme will serve as possible research material.

4. Assign additional research assignments
Challenge your students to find additional evidence that may support or negate a generalization or to relate the theme to a topic that especially interests them.

5. Brief parents on the themes you will teach
Parents need to be made aware of the complex learning that will occur in your classroom so they can better assist their children when they come home with questions or assignments related to the theme. Have formal after-school meetings with parents or send letters home explaining the thematic unit.

6. Assign homework related to the theme
Since parents will be made aware of the themes being studied, it is a great idea to have your students work with their family on a project at home. For example, in studying the pioneers and "Adaptation," I asked my students and their parents to write an essay detailing how pioneers adapted to traveling by wagon.

7. Know your learners
In choosing your themes it is a good idea to consider the population you have in your classroom. For example, because of the high transiency rate in my school and classroom it was very appropriate and useful for me to pick "Change" and "Adaptation" as my themes.

8. Keep an open mind
Listen to what the children have to say. Because themes are universal, studying them brings up many different points of view. Do not be afraid to follow a different path to which your students may lead.

9. Do not feel pressured to include all subjects
If you cannot include seven subject areas into your plan, do not give up on thematic instruction. Remember that if you're able to incorporate at least three of the disciplines you will do great.

10. Team Teach
Few things can make your life easier as a teacher than team teaching. Remember that two heads are always better than one.

Reader Reflections

Insights: _____

_____

_____

_____

_____

_____

Actions for Our School (District) to Consider: _____

_____

_____

_____

_____

_____

_____

_____

COMMUNITY TREASURE HUNT

Here's how this teacher canvassed the community to get free resources for her classroom.

4

My classroom is humming with activity as students hurry to complete their science experiments. In one corner of the room, several students are working on an electricity experiment with coated copper wire and light bulbs. In the opposite corner, students are testing pieces of styrofoam with various solvents, to determine which are biodegradable and which are non-biodegradable. At still another workstation, students are taping X-rays together to make a skeleton. The rest of my students are gathered around a plastic terrarium, feeding shredded newspapers, fruit peelings, and eggshells to earthworms.

What's amazing about this busy scene is that textbooks were the only science supplies we had at the start of the school year! So where did all these materials and equipment come from? Everything—from the earthworms to the X-rays—was donated to my classroom by various businesses in the community.

I teach second grade at Skyline Heights Elementary School in Harrison, Arkansas. Even though we have a talented, creative staff who work very well together, our school doesn't always have the funds for the extra supplies we need to support and enhance the curriculum. We're part of a small school district in a rural community, with a total enrollment of 2,800 students. My school, one of five elementary schools in the district, serves 400 children in grades K-4.

Harrison, a community of approximately 11,000 people, is

JOAN REID
Grade 2
Skyline Heights
Elementary School
Harrison, Arkansas

THE ULTIMATE BEGINNER'S GUIDE 49

situated in the middle of the Ozarks in Boone County. Even though Harrison is small, it has a diversified economy that includes industry, tourism, retail sales, and agriculture. Our students and their families have access to many recreational areas and cultural activities, including lakes, rivers, parks, theaters, and museums.

At Skyline Heights, we believe our students benefit from a combination of varied cultural activities and diverse school experiences. We also believe we must provide a learning environment that enables all

Parents are our greatest resource.

children to reach their potential. In my classroom, I work to create an environment that will adapt to the needs of all my students while encouraging their desire to learn. I need an abundance of resources, however, to design a classroom environment conducive to active participation for all my students.

Taking Stock

When I first surveyed my room, I quickly realized that, beyond textbooks and paper, I didn't have very much equipment. We were lacking science and math manipulatives, such as syringes and plastic tubing for air pressure experiments, beans for counting, and clear containers for storage. We also needed extra paintbrushes, sponges, yarn, potting soil, clothespins, and a host of other items to use in experiments.

It was obvious to me that we needed more money. I knew the funds and resources were out there. It was just a matter of getting to them. My co-workers and I met with Cathy Ramsey, our principal, and we began to make a list of supplies we required for the school year. We first went through our science books and listed all the equipment we needed for experiments.

Parents as a Resource

Our next step was to share our list with the students' parents. Parents are our greatest resource, and they often approach businesses for us. One of our parents arranged for a local business, Miller's Hardware, to donate the supplies we needed for our experiments. The store donated Elmer's glue, batteries, copper wire, flashlights, and disposable plastic gloves. Whenever we need to replenish our supplies, we give the hardware store a list of items.

Another parent arranged for Edwards Grocery to give us their damaged goods once a month. We use these items— sugar cubes, macaroni noodles, vinegar, baking soda—for science experiments and other projects.

Wishing Trees

Parents help make the rest of our wishes come true as well. At the annual open house at the start of the school year, each teacher puts a "wishing tree" on the chalkboard, with 25 paper apples on the branches. Written on each apple is a "wish" or "want" for that year, such as computer games, seeds for experiments, paper for art, school supplies, Polaroid film, or "your pick." Each parent takes an "apple" and sometime during the year, that parent sends the item to school.

Our wishing trees have been a great success. My classroom has received some wonderful surprise items. My first year we actually got a computer in exchange for an "apple." One year, my request for bags for students to put their work in led to a gift of 400 white sacks from the Pippin Wholesale Company. I was able to distribute them throughout the entire school.

A parent who worked at a Shelby's, a local gift store, sent us large quantities of styrofoam packing chips, which we used for various science experiments.

Another parent who works at Millbrook, a local distributor with lots of paper products, called to see if we could use paper in two sizes. The principal and I went there after school and loaded my car with bolts of drawing and writing paper for the entire year! Millbrook told us it would help them if we could do this on a regular basis. So we worked out a pick-up schedule that keeps the school constantly supplied with paper.

In addition to the wishing tree, we also send a letter to parents with a list of items that can be found in their homes: ribbon, lace, buttons, beans, plastic containers, tongue depressors, wall-paper scraps, old cards, etc. By October, we review our wish lists to see what we have received. Usually we have been successful in most areas.

Adopt-a-Class

Parents also play a key role in our Adopt-a-Class program. Many people have heard of Adopt-a-School programs, where a business or organization partners with a school, providing monetary assistance and other types of support. At

We loaded my car with bolts of drawing and writing paper for the entire year!

Skyline Heights, we've given this concept a new twist. Our

Adopt-a-Class program helps individual teachers bear the costs for classroom extras such as markers, art projects, or computer games.

If you don't ask, you won't get anything!

We send a note home with each student, asking parents or grandparents if they would like to "adopt" their child's class for a month. The note reminds parents that teachers often spend a lot of money out of their own pockets to furbish their classrooms and augment their lessons. Adopt-a-Class is an easy, inexpensive way for individual parents to contribute to the classroom fund. If parents are interested, they pay ten dollars to adopt our class for one month. We send out reminders to the parents during the month they have chosen, and the child brings in the check, money order, or cash the next day.

Approaching the Business Community

Our motto is "If you don't ask, you won't get anything!" We've asked local businesses to donate to our school, and the response has been overwhelmingly positive. When you approach businesses in your area, keep the following information in mind.

Make Contact

Start with businesses you patronize. If you spend your money there, you're a valued customer and they are more likely to say "yes" to your requests. If you're not a patron, try to find someone (parent, teacher, administrator, neighbor) who is. Have this person approach the business for you. If they are not able to do so, have them give you the name of a contact. When you're ready to ask for a donation, make a personal visit. Try not to rely on phone calls or letters; it's usually better to have face-to-face contact.

Be Specific

When asking for something you need, be as specific as possible. Don't just walk in and ask if they have something they want to contribute to your school. Bring a note or flyer on school stationery that lists what you need. Talk to the people who work there about the items on your list. Tell them what you are trying to achieve in your school or classroom. Let them know what the students are studying and how you will use their donations. Not only will they appreciate knowing how their money or merchandise will be used, your information will help them identify the nature of their donations if they have to fill out a form for their parent company or national office at the end of the fiscal year.

Make It Easy

Once a business has agreed to donate something, ask them about a convenient pick-up time. If they are giving you a lot of free merchandise, they may not want their other customers to see you walking out with it—especially during their busy hours. If possible, arrange to make the pick-up yourself instead of sending a co-worker or representative. As soon as you get the merchandise back to your classroom, start working on a thank-you note. Always send thank-you notes within two weeks, and try to deliver them personally.

Types of Donations

Local businesses often need direction and suggestions about the ways in which they can make meaningful contributions. Businesses can contribute to schools in a myriad of ways, from participating in fundraising events, to giving out certificates for free merchandise, to donating items they are unable to sell. For instance, grocery stores often have damaged goods and perishable items they ordinarily would just throw away. However, your school may be able to use these items for a variety of projects. We've used slightly squashed sheet cakes for math lessons on fractions, day-old bread that we mix with Elmer's glue and water to make playdough or clay, and damaged ice-cream cones for geometry lessons.

Area hospitals can also be a good place to get resources for your classroom. After my son had several X-rays taken because of sports injuries, I came up with the idea of collecting the entire skeleton. My dentist and doctor told me to check with our local hospital, the Northwest Arkansas Regional Medical Center. When I spoke to the X-ray technician, I found out that January is the "clean-out" month for hospital X-rays. After the patients' names are removed from the X-rays, I go and pick up stacks of them. Then I sort the X-rays into skeletons, and I distribute them to the rest of the faculty.

Tips for Getting Donations

- Unless they offer, don't "hit" the same businesses twice for the same stuff.

- Some teachers are not "high profile" or comfortable asking for free materials. Don't make them. Find other ways to involve them in the process.

- When putting together a team of people to work on a project, make sure it's a flexible group that can put in some time. Always include two or three "go-getters" who have the energy and enthusiasm to make the event a success.

- Lots of businesses get approached by various groups in the community. If you call a business and they say they've already given, don't just say okay and hang up. Thank them for giving to the community, tell them to remember your school if they ever have merchandise to discard. Ask them what the school and students can do for them. Can you volunteer to do a task for them? Would they like students' artwork or stories to display on their walls?

The X-rays make a wonderful science or health lesson. Using tape, students assemble the individual charts into an entire skeleton. They attach the skeletons to the large picture windows in our classroom, where the sunlight can shine through them. We use them to study cloudy lungs, guess body weights, measure bones, and examine breaks and

A perfect time to ask for a donation is when you're making a purchase.

fractures. The X-rays are also an excellent alternative to the typical Halloween fare. In addition, the students are so fascinated that playground injuries actually decrease by using these lessons.

Getting Donations for Fund-Raisers

Octoberfest

The success of Octoberfest, our largest annual fund-raiser, is due in large part to the support we receive from local businesses. Thanks to our benefactors, we've auctioned off a surprising variety of items, including flower arrangements, mugs with store logos, food and video coupons, furniture, pet grooming services, oil changes, gasoline, haircuts and hair coloring, boating supplies, birthday parties, clothing, accessories, radios, sporting equipment signed by a football player, golf shirts, meals at local restaurants, toys, and artwork.

Some businesses will donate big ticket items such as a boat or jet skis at cost, which means the school pays the store only what they originally paid for the item. We get to auction the item off at a higher price and keep the profit. Also, we don't have to pay for food for the fund-raiser because all the food and drinks are donated by local restaurants.

We start preparing for Octoberfest by holding a meeting and asking teachers to make a list of the businesses they would like to ask for donations of prizes and silent auction items. If some teachers don't feel comfortable approaching businesses for donations, we give them other jobs to do. After we complete our lists, we compare them to avoid duplicating our efforts. Then we go into the community to solicit donations for the fund-raiser. We also put up a marquee outside the school advertising the fund-raiser and asking for donations.

How To Solicit a Donation

A perfect time to ask for a donation is when you're making a purchase! When I was getting gas from the Main Street Exxon gas station one morning, I initiated a conversation with the station manager about my school's Octoberfest fund-raiser. I asked whether the station would consider donating free gasoline or an oil change for our silent auction. Even though his daughter's school was giving a fund-raiser around the same time, the manager generously gave me a gift certificate. I used the same technique to get golf shirts from Golf Etc. I was spending money at the store, having my golf shoes fixed. I noticed the sales rack was full and asked the manager if he was having trouble selling the golf shirts. I asked him if he wanted to donate one for our silent auction, and he told me to go on over and pick out the one I wanted.

Approaching New Businesses

In addition to asking the stores we patronize for donations, we always check with the new businesses in the community. They can really benefit from the advertising and good public relations. If I don't know anyone at a business and have never been there before, I might send them a letter instead of walking in "cold."

The letter, written on school stationery and signed by the principal or PTA president, states that we would like to advertise their business at our next fund-raiser. We ask whether they have small items they would like to donate—such as ink pads, pens, and pencils inscribed with the name of the business. (Even though we ask for a modest donation, we often end up getting something really good.) I end the letter by telling them I will contact them on a specific date. If they don't wish to contribute when I call, I ask them if I may contact them again next year.

Thanks to the support of parents and local businesses, our fund-raisers are a great success. Last year, we held a talent contest with the local disc jockey

Even though we ask stores for modest donations, we often end up getting something really good.

(one of our parents) as master of ceremonies. Our biggest draw was the softball throw in which a policeman (also a parent) used a radar gun to mark the speed of the ball. We raised $3,000 and Walmart gave us a $2,000 matching grant, so the fund-raiser brought in a total of $5,000. We always divide the profits from the Octoberfest between the teachers and the PTA. The money is used for items such as

Matching Grants

In addition to free materials, grants are an excellent way of getting additional resources for your school. The money from many of our fund-raisers has been doubled by matching funds grants that we've gotten from Walmart. Walmart has a wonderful grant that will match the money a school raises up to $2,000. Not a lot of people know about it, but it's an excellent "starter" grant because it's so easy to apply for. It's just a half a page and it's simple to fill out. Walmart's matching funds grant application is due in January of each year, and you can pick it up from any Walmart service center. Walmart has other education grants: a $250 teacher foundation award and an environmental grant for $300 dollars if a school reduces, reuses, and recycles.

computers, educational games, and playground equipment.

Read-a-thon

We used our community connections to get prizes for our Read-a-thon fund-raiser as well. It's sponsored by the PTA to help pay for an ongoing playground equipment project. Students read for two weeks and they're paid a penny or a nickel a page. Prizes for the Read-a-thon are donated from a variety of area businesses: Breadoux Pizza, McDonalds, Burger King, Mall Cinema, Vision Video, Hardys, Taco Bell, Sports and Moore, Miller's Hardware, Golf Etc., and TCBY. They provide free merchandise, gift certificates, and/or money. We use parents as contacts to get these donations.

My husband works at Miller's Hardware, the McDonalds' community relations representative is a parent at our school, and one of the PTA fathers is a manager at the Mall Cinema. Vision Video has been donating movie rentals to Read-a-thon for about six years, ever since a parent who works for the store brought them on board. Six years ago, I asked Sports and Moore Athletic Shop to donate hats and T-shirts for our fund-raiser, and they've participated every year since. With a matching funds grant from Walmart, Read-a-thon generated about $4,000 for our school last year.

How We Give Back

Our school has been fortunate to get a tremendous amount of products and services from our community, so it's important we show our appreciation and give something in return. We always send handwritten thank-you letters to each of our benefactors, and next year, we're thinking about listing "thank yous" in our local paper as well. The school newsletter is another venue we use to list and thank our sponsors. And we remind faculty to thank people personally whenever they patronize a store, restaurant, or other business that has donated to the school.

We also have students show benefactors our appreciation. For instance, our school has worked out a mutually beneficial arrangement with McDonalds, Burger King, and Taco Bell. These restaurants give us free food certificates to pass out as classroom incentives. In return, our students create new artwork each month, which is hung on the walls of these restaurants. You can't just expect businesses to keep handing over their resources. It's important to reciprocate whenever possible.

There are other meaningful ways in which our students give back to the community. School projects include: "Big Help," a one-month donation drive for the Sanctuary; a pet food drive for the Humane Society; a winter coat drive for children and adults without coats; and a "Share and Care" canned food drive before Christmas.

My students also make holiday cards for hospice and hospital patients, which I deliver each month. In the spring, we present a program of poetry and song for Hospice Day. This program is videotaped by our librarian and given to hospice patients and the local television station to share with the public, particularly parents and grandparents who couldn't attend.

Resource Workshops

My colleagues and I have gained so much experience hunting down free resources that we were asked to give a workshop on the subject for other teachers in the community. The workshop, sponsored by the Educational Resource Center Cooperative, was a two-night session complete with dinner.

We began by telling participants (local science and math teachers) that we had discovered many ways to obtain free resources for our classrooms and that we had used some of these very resources to put together the workshop. We shared the names of the sponsors who had donated materials to the workshop. Then we discussed the methods for approaching businesses described earlier in this chapter.

We had loads of free stuff to give the teachers (which, incidentally, was great advertising for the businesses that had donated materials for the workshop). We had note pads from banks, pens and pencils with names of businesses, Farm Bureau free materials, birdhouses, seeds, Baggies™, sugar cubes, balloons, salt and pepper, lemon juice, copper wire, corks, light bulbs, flashlights, books, and eye charts. All of these materials could be used for the science and math activities in our textbooks.

Students' artwork is hung on the walls of restaurants.

Even our dinner was donated by local merchants. The meal—which had a math theme—

included a huge sub sandwich donated by Subway. We used a yardstick donated by Miller's Hardware to measure the sandwich for slicing. Dessert was ice cream cones and scoops of ice cream from Edward's Grocery. The paper plates and utensils for our meal also came from Miller Hardware. The store had purchased a huge consignment bin containing paper plates, napkins, plastic utensils, and even salt and pepper packages. We had practically everything we needed in one box.

Free resources—money or materials—can make all the difference in your school and classroom, but these extras aren't totally "free." They require time, effort, and the willingness to form partnerships within the community. The benefits are more than worth it, however, and the process can be a lot of fun. Our school is very lucky to have such a strong coalition among teachers, administrators, parents, and local business people. In order to get the best for our students, our staff works overtime and goes that extra mile to empower our students to become life-long learners in a rapidly changing society.

> *Getting free resources requires the willingness to form partnerships within the community.*

How To Get Grants and Free Stuff Reproducible 4.1

Advice on Forming Community Partnerships

- Join teacher and community organizations.

- Enter local and state contests.

- Bring in speakers from local industries to talk or read to your class.

- Take pictures of students participating in various school and classroom activities, and deliver them to your local newspaper.

- Nurture ties with alumni (our high school library receives money each year from a retired person in the community).

- Always write thank-you notes.

- After a fund-raiser, list all donations in the school newsletter or newspaper.

How To Get Grants and Free Stuff Reproducible 4.2

Adopt-a-Class

Would you be willing to adopt a class? Funding to schools is limited. Teachers use a lot of their own money for many of the stickers, special art projects, awards, and incentive prizes the children love. To help with these costs, the PTA provides the Adopt-a-Class program. Parents may adopt a class for $10 a month. You may adopt as many classes as you wish, with all proceeds going to the classroom. You will receive an official adoption paper from your adopted classroom. This is a great way for parents to get involved and help teachers, too!

Thank you for your support.
Skyline Heights PTA

Yes, I would like to Adopt-a-Class!

Name _____

Class(es) _____

Month(s) _____

Check One: ☐ I am enclosing $10.00 for month adopted.

☐ Bill me when it's my month.

Reader Reflections

Ideas for Grant Projects: _____

_____

_____

_____

Possible Funding Sources: _____

_____

_____

_____

Community Contacts for Free Resources: _____

_____

_____

_____

Teacher Review

Multiple Intelligences

WEATHERING MULTIPLE INTELLIGENCES

Before I began teaching, I had an image in my mind of my future classroom. All of the students would be sitting up straight in their desks, diligently listening and asking questions, soaking up the information and becoming excited about learning.

It took all of ten minutes my first day in a sixth grade Language Arts classroom to realize that I had been seriously deluded. I was faced with a room full of very different children, each with his or her own special learning style. It was obvious that the same approach would not work with everyone. "Weathering Multiple Intelligences" expertly illustrates many of the methods and activities that I find especially useful when trying to access those many different learning styles.

Kendall and Harless suggest a variety of activities that I have implemented in some fashion in my Language Arts lessons. When teaching new vocabulary, I, too, use art and movement to help students remember the definitions. Students look up the words in a dictionary, brainstorm in teams to find synonyms, create webs, develop movements to go along with the definitions, and draw pictures to symbolize meaning. Using these methods, I have discovered that, overall, students are more successful on tests and truly understand the meaning of the words. They often tell me when they have encountered one of our words outside the classroom setting.

Although Kendall and Harless use a unit on weather as a means of illustrating multiple intelligence activities, their basic ideas and messages are easily integrated into a wide range of subject areas. In addition, I will definitely be using their thematic unit planning guide and self-evaluation form to insure that I never overlook the unique needs of each student.

Catherine A. Dietz
Language Arts Teacher
Somerville Junior High School
Somerville, Texas

WEATHERING MULTIPLE INTELLIGENCES

An integrated thematic unit on weather proved ripe with opportunities to address multiple intelligences.

Anyone who has worked with thematic units knows how much work—and how much fun—they can be. Well it's even better when you add multiple intelligences activities to thematic units. That's what we did in our classes at Hillcrest Elementary School in Oak Harbor, Washington. I have 15 years of experience teaching kids in grades kindergarten through fifth grade. My partner, Shirley Harless, has been teaching for ten years in grades one through five.

Oak Harbor is located on the northern part of Whidbey Island in Washington state. The Whidbey Island Naval Air Station is located in the area, and approximately 60 percent of our students have parents who serve in the Navy. These students generally stay in our area from two to five years. Our school district has six elementary schools, ranging in size from 300 to 600 students each. There are also two middle schools and one high school.

BARBARA KENDALL and SHIRLEY HARLESS
Hillcrest Elementary School
Oak Harbor, Washington

When Opportunity Knocks...

Each year our school district gives four science kits to classes in grade levels K-7. During my second year as a third grade teacher, I noticed that Shirley Harless, who teaches fifth grade, received a science kit with a topic similar to mine. The topic was weather. We talked that year about planning some activities that would allow our third and fifth grade students to work together on weather-related projects. We saw this as a precursor to implementing a cross-age curriculum. We decided an integrated curriculum around the theme of weather would be the best way to do this.

Both of us attended a workshop to help plan the thematic unit. As we began creating our integrated unit, we learned of a short course introducing the theory of multiple intelligences. That course left us wanting more information. We later received support from our principal to attend a three-day conference on multiple intelligences.

During this conference, we had the opportunity to listen to Dr. Howard Gardner on three different occasions as he spoke about his experiences using multiple intelligences as a means to instruct students. Other presenters, including Linda Campbell from Antioch University, Dee Dickinson of New Horizons For Learning, and Nancy Skerritt, a curriculum specialist in Takoma School District #409, presented the different categories of multiple intelligences.

We left the conference excited and ready to get started using multiple intelligence activities within our integrated unit on weather. Our goal was to implement this within a cross-age setting, using our third and fifth graders. We hoped to improve our methods of teaching and provide students with multiple ways of learning.

We knew our thematic unit on weather would be filled with lots of rich activities for students. But linking those activities to each of the seven intelligences would accommodate a variety of learning styles and strengths in the classroom.

We hoped to provide students with multiple ways of learning.

Getting a Head Start on Planning

We learned about multiple intelligences at the end of May. We decided to implement our weather unit in the fall. But we wanted to begin planning for fall during the early part of the summer. This would allow us to use the bulk of the summer to gather materials and revise plans as needed.

During the first two weeks after school was out for the summer, we gathered information on activities our kids could do that related to weather. We had our science kits from the district, but we wanted to supplement the kits with other activities.

We started to plan by deciding how many weeks we wanted the unit to last. We decided to aim for a nine-week instructional program.

We also had to figure out how much of our time would be spent in a cross-age setting. Previously, we had agreed that some class time would be cross-age, while students would remain with their primary class for other activities. We structured the program so that our third and fifth graders would spend at least one to 1-1/2 hours each week together in cross-age activities. The remainder of the time would be used for self-contained activities. But we decided to remain flexible throughout and change plans when necessary.

Creating Multiple Intelligences Activities

As I mentioned earlier, we wanted the learning activities within our weather unit to relate to each of the seven intelligences. To help us keep track of each activity, we took a large sheet of butcher paper and divided it into seven sections for the each of the intelligences: The sections were labeled verbal/linguistic, logical/mathematical, visual/spatial, bodily/kinesthetic, musical, interpersonal, and intrapersonal. Next, we began to create a list of activities that third and fifth graders could work on together, along with tasks students could perform within their own classrooms. These activities all had to be related to our weather theme.

Cross-Age Activities

The unit began with an introduction to the water cycle for third graders. Fifth graders received a shorter review of the topic. Students reviewed this material in their individual classrooms. Later that week, we began to create cross-age groups. We separated students into groups of four. Each group contained two third graders and two fifth grade students. Students met within their groups, and were instructed to brainstorm a list of weather-related words. The words most frequently mentioned were sunny, rainy, cloudy, windy, snowy, and calm.

Then, the children were asked to sit in their groups and make a chart of the words, along with a list of activities to do during each kind of weather.

This exercise served as a great ground-breaker. It gave the children a chance to get to know each other and begin working together. The exercise gave us teachers an opportunity to watch the children working together and to give some specific guidance in cooperative learning. Also, the cooperative learning groups were great activities for students who are strong in interpersonal intelligence.

As the final part of this lesson, each child was given the opportunity to choose one of the kinds of weather and write about their favorite activity to do on that kind of weather day.

Charting and Graphing the Weather

During the second week of the unit, we introduced the concept of a monthly weather calendar. On that calendar, students would keep track of the weather each day by using specific symbols. At the end of each month, the students would take all of their information from the calendar and process it into graphs. The graphs would be kept for comparing the weather this particular year, to other years. The charting and graphing exercises allowed us to explore students logical/

Lessons Learned

Here are some important lessons we learned that may serve you well if you start a unit like this:

1. Find a partner with similar expectations regarding behavior, openness to change, goals. Flexibility is important!
2. Plan ahead. Give yourselves enough time to change your mind.
3. Create an open learning environment.
4. Include other staff members who show an interest.
5. Feel comfortable with "noisy learning." Activities using multiple intelligences are not necessarily quiet.
6. Enlist the aid of a specialist in the subject area (in this case a weather expert).
7. Use trays or tubs to set up stations quickly. Provide the children with instructions that they can read and follow to build their experiments.
8. Build the instruments yourself first. It helps to anticipate some of the problems which may occur.
9. Use alternative assessment techniques including observation, open-ended questioning, and student self-assessment.
10. Accept student ideas to amend instruments. They sometimes work better.

mathematical intelligence activities.

Reading and Writing About Weather

We then read the book *It Looked Like Spilt Milk* to the whole group of third and fifth graders. The book talks about various cloud formations. After the reading, students went back to their individual classrooms and built clouds. Third graders used paint blown by straws to create their clouds, while fifth graders used torn pieces of paper.

In the third grade class, we had students complete the sentence, "It looked like _____." At the same time, fifth grade students wrote a paragraph about their cloud art project. These art projects were later displayed in the school hallway. During this week we also had students work on cloud formations and vocabulary development.

The art projects allow students to express their visual/spatial intelligence. Writing and vocabulary exercises brought out students' verbal/linguistic intelligence.

Creating Weather Instruments

By the third week, we were ready to build weather instruments. The weather instruments were a crucial part of the unit. Students would use these instruments throughout the unit to gather data about various types of weather.

We collected simple instructions and diagrams that we enlarged and laminated for the children to use in building their instruments. For this activity, students worked in their cross-age groups. We received help from one instruction assistant, two parent volunteers, and one high school teaching assistant.

We required students to read the instructions for assembling each weather instrument, make measurements, label projects, and assemble parts. We worked on these projects for three weeks (weeks three, four and five of the unit). Students built wind vanes, hygrometers, rain gauges, barometers, anemometers, and Cartesian divers.

Creating weather instruments gave us a chance to incorporate activities around a number of the intelligences. Students had to read instructions, assemble parts, and work as a team. All of these tasks allowed kids to express their particular learning style or intelligence. For example, kids prone to more verbal/linguistic intelligence could easily read the assembly instructions. Following diagrams worked well for our visual/spatial learners. The teamwork encouraged interpersonal intelligence. The actual building and assembly of the weather instruments brought out bodily/kinesthetic intelligences.

When students finished building each instrument we asked them to fill out a form with the following information: What did I build? What does it mea-

We decided to remain flexible throughout, and change plans when necessary.

sure or simulate? What materials did I use? and How can this instrument tell me more about the weather?

We originally intended this activity to take two weeks. We soon realized this was much too rapid an assignment for our students. So we added the third week for construction.

Creating Rhythm Instruments

During the fourth week we had students build a simple rhythm instrument as a homework assignment. We found some simple instructions and displayed them in the classroom for students to follow.

Each child was given a sticky note to write their name on. Students attached their name to the instrument they wanted to build. We then made copies of the directions for construction of these instruments and gave them to each student to take home. Students had two weeks to complete this homework assignment. We ended up with a wonderful variety of rhythm instruments.

We decided to use those instruments during week six of our unit. That week, we gave a lesson on creating rhythms. Students worked together to create a rhythm expressing a form of weather. They then presented their rhythm to the entire group. At the end of this lesson, we asked students to think about a movement which would fit with each rhythm. The movements simulated some kind of weather from tornadoes to hurricanes.

At the beginning of week seven, we continued to use some of the rhythms created by students. For example, we formed a large circle and performed rhythms (in a wave format) that illustrated a rainstorm from beginning to end.

Not only were our music and movement activities theme-related, they emphasized students' musical and bodily/kinesthetic intelligences.

During the seventh week, we again brainstormed weather words. It was amazing to us how much vocabulary the kids had learned. Students got a chance to put that vocabulary to good use when we asked them to work together in mixed-age groups to create weather-related poetry.

Putting it All Together

We reached week eight and decided to combine the rhythms, movement, and poetry into one major performance. We gave students time during week eight and week nine to get ready for the production.

It was amazing to us how much vocabulary the kids had learned.

It was during week nine that students gave their performance before several other classrooms. The production was certainly not up to the New York stage level, but the children had created it on their own, and the response by the other children in the school was good. We videotaped this performance and talked with the children about it later.

Our music teacher joined our group and gathered material for a program about the weather which the children performed for their parents. This performance also included singing, dancing, and speaking parts, along with rhythm instruments.

Weather on The Internet

We looked for, and found, opportunities to use technology within our unit. We applied for, and received, a state grant to use the Internet as part of our weather unit. Students logged onto the Internet through our Educational Service District's Internet node. They used the Internet to send and receive weather information from other schools in Washington, Idaho, and Oregon.

We kept students in their cross-age groups while working on the computers. Before they got started, we taught each group how to long-on, send data, and ask intelligent questions. We also showed students how to cut, copy, and paste text. One cross-age group met each morning at 8:30 a.m. to surf the Internet. The students used their previously built weather instruments to collect data about the weather. The collected data was sent to other schools on-line.

The first of group of students we trained quickly became experts and assisted other groups as they used the Internet. Each student within the group had a turn at logging-on and sending data.

The initial purpose for using the Internet was to share with other schools, some weather data that we could chart and graph. But while we were online, many exciting opportunities emerged for further learning.

As an introductory step, the students played a game of 20 Questions with the participating schools. Our students tried to determine the location and grade level of the students from other schools on-line. We had students use maps to locate their on-line friends. Well, this helped students become attuned to the geography of the Northwest. They subsequently researched mining records, dams, and topographic maps about each geographic area.

Using the Internet afforded great opportunities for cooperative learning and interpersonal intelligence. Older students showed their younger peers how to use maps and how to ask questions on-line. In essence, students were working together with interest and accomplishment, regardless of age or skill level.

Once we got students going on the Internet, we monitored their work with only occasional troubleshooting of Internet problems. We found that students had begun working independently and were competent enough using the computer to know when they really needed help. This portion of our unit was highly successful.

The only problem of consequence was with our school connections. Some of the schools lost their Internet connection due to

We found opportunities to use technology within our unit.

a lack of funding. We posted a request for more participating schools on the State computer bulletin board while continuing on-line with other participating schools.

We have since begun to work in advance to post on the State bulletin board to find out if there are any interested teachers/schools/districts.

Project Evaluation

We evaluated our work as we went along. We took time to jot down ideas and share thoughts about the unit, during activities and at the end of each day. The children moved between our classrooms in a well-behaved fashion, without a great deal of discipline required. The children seemed to enjoy the various groupings that allowed them to work with each other. Parents were happy to be involved in our activities and helped out whenever asked. Our administrator supported our requests for training and enjoyed our programs and student presentations.

We were able to find and create activities corresponding to each of the seven intelligences within our weather unit. We believe this led to a rich learning experience where each student's learning style and strength was encouraged.

Future Plans

We are always refining our weather unit and continue to look for opportunities to add further multiple intelligence activities. We are now using multiple intelligence activities in a cross-age setting, within a science unit on animals. This unit has been expanded to include a fourth grade class.

Multiple Intelligences Reproducible 5.1

Thematic Unit Planning with the Multiple Intelligences

Unit Title: _____

Unit Objective(s): _____

    Learning Activities: _____

        Verbal/Linguistic: _____

        Logical/Mathematical: _____

        Visual/Spatial: _____

        Bodily/Kinesthetic: _____

        Musical: _____

        Interpersonal: _____

        Intrapersonal: _____

Unit Sequence: _____

Assessment Procedures: _____

Materials/Resources Needed: _____

Multiple Intelligences Reproducible 5.2

Multiple Intelligences Activities for Weather Unit

Intelligence	Activities
Verbal/Linguistic	Read the book *It Looked Like Spilt Milk*. Write sentences finishing the phrase "It Looked Like_____"
Logical/Mathematical	Draw a diagram of the water cycle. Create a monthly weather calendar. Create a graph showing weather patterns during the month. Analyze collected weather data.
Visual/Spatial	Create a collage of pictures showing different types of weather. Display data as graphs and charts.
Bodily/Kinesthetic	Create a weather dance pleasing or asking the weather spirits. Build weather instruments.
Musical	Research and build different types of percussion instruments. Create a rhythm and teach it to others. Create a song using weather words and concepts.
Interpersonal	Work together in groups to build instruments, collect data, perform songs.
Intrapersonal	Keep a journal of weather-related activities. List your favorite things to do on different weather days.

Multiple Intelligences Reproducible 5.3

Self-Evaluation for Weather Theme Unit

Name: _____

I Learned: _____

_____

I Made: _____

_____

I Wrote: _____

_____

I Read: _____

_____

The Best Part Was: _____

_____

My Best Work Was: _____

_____

Reader Reflections

Insights: _____

_____

_____

_____

_____

Actions for Our School (District) to Consider: _____

_____

_____

_____

_____

_____

_____

Teacher Review

Teaching with Technology

WIRED FOR BETTER WRITING

In "Wired for Better Writing," Beth Cristensen, an 8th grade English teacher, outlines how the use of a word processor, the Internet, and a package called Claris-Works Home Page helps her students strengthen their writing, reading, and critical thinking skills. I've used word processors and the Internet in similar fashion in my own classes, and I found that Cristensen's information helped me to come up with new strategies for my own teaching.

Cristensen begins by stressing the importance of basic communication skills. I echo her sentiments! Regardless of technology, students will always need the ability to read and think critically. They will also need sound writing skills. By using a word processing package, students can hone every aspect of the writing process, from brainstorm to final draft. Word processing makes for more logical and cohesive writing, and this skill is crucial to all disciplines. And, like Cristensen's, my students are enthralled by the Internet. Many of them will surf forever, finding both useful and not so useful information for school projects. Meanwhile, while surfing the net, and without feeling as if they are working, students are practicing reasoning and critical thinking skills. That's smart shopping!

As in Cristensen's classes, my student Web pages provide a format for engaging peer evaluation. They encourage students to be meticulous in their writing, since their work will be posted for the whole world to see. In my 9th grade English classes, student Web pages help to "raise the bar" in student writing on small and large projects. I can also use my class Web page to post homework information, reminders, and links to valuable resources for projects we create in class. In reading Cristensen's narrative, I am encouraged to remember that implementing technology does not have to be a threatening and onerous task—it can actually make teaching easier.

Josette Darden
English Teacher
James Hubert Blake High School
Silver Spring, MD

WIRED FOR BETTER WRITING

Computer technology has dramatically increased the level of effort these eighth grade students put into their writing.

6 Seven short years ago, turning on a computer was a terrifying experience for me. Today, personal computers and the Internet are critical to the way I teach eighth grade English. They have also dramatically increased the level of effort my students put into their writing, which now enjoys, thanks to the Internet, a national—indeed an international—audience. The integration of technology into my teaching not only helps my students master basic English skills, it also expands their horizons and prepares them to function effectively in the information age.

For over 25 years, I've taught English to eighth graders in the Mankato area of Minnesota, the state's south central economic center. Mankato is a middle-class community of 31,000 with a

BETH CRISTENSEN
Dakota Meadows
Middle School
North Mankato, Minnesota

minority population that is less than five percent. Most of our students continue their education beyond high school. Before 1993, I taught at Mankato West High School, where overcrowding provided the impetus to develop a separate middle school for grades seven and eight.

The use of personal computer technology is one of the distinguishing features that grew out of the planning effort for Dakota Meadows Middle School. Our broad-based planning team of teachers, administrators, and community members also opted for a "house" system, strong

THE ULTIMATE BEGINNER'S GUIDE 75

student/faculty advisor relationships, and an emphasis on learning by doing.

Our school is organized into "houses" that are named after

> *We underestimated the constant demand that computer technology creates for cash.*

Native American trails. I teach English to the 160 students in the Minneopa House. The purpose of our houses is to provide the intimate learning environment of small schools within our larger school. The Native American names reflect the importance of the Native American tradition to our school and community.

In the late 1980s, while Dakota Meadows was being planned, personal computers began to dot the workplace, and we knew it was only a matter of time before parents and students would expect computers in the schools. After visiting other new schools, the planning team made a commitment to integrate computer technology into the school from the start. Fiscal tradeoffs were, of course, necessary. The physical plant was scaled back to shift money into wiring the school for the future. We chose cyberspace over physical space, opting for televisions and at least one computer in each classroom.

In the Beginning

We started small, with one computer lab and high hopes for more. But we underestimated the constant demand that computer technology creates for cash. Web sites require increased memory, and new software programs require increased speed. So upgrading computers is a frequent necessity. Fortunately, support from parents has made it possible for our school to sustain a commitment to technology despite fluctuating budgets. We depend on money raised by our parent-teacher organization's annual magazine sale to supplement whatever funds the school district provides. We now have two computer labs connected to the Internet, one of which is equipped with the versatile Macintosh G3s. We also have two word-processing labs and a computer in every classroom.

The integration of technology into our school created two formidable challenges. One, finding enough cash for our technology needs, will always be with us. The other, bringing our faculty and staff into the information age, we have successfully overcome.

When our new school first opened, there were people who said, "I'll never, never use a computer." And there were some who dragged their feet the first year. But there's not a person now who's not computer-competent. Anyone who works in our building in any capacity—teachers, aides, cooks, janitors, electricians, full- or part-time—has an E-mail account. And anyone who works full-time has his or her own computer. Our principal uses E-mail to communicate with teachers. Faculty circulate, via E-mail, the "minutes" from house meetings to appropriate colleagues. And every year, all of us use E-mail more and more to communicate with parents. There are real advantages to being able to contact parents without the hassle of finding the right time for a telephone call.

My Personal Technology Odyssey

In 1992, I wrote a grant for my first computer. I tried to think of it as no more than a sophisticated typewriter. But when it arrived, I was so afraid that I didn't even hook it up. My nine-year-old daughter did!

Libby taught me how to use the computer at home. She was also my tutor during the six-week computer training course for district teachers in our area. Every week, on the afternoon of the course, I picked Libby up from elementary school and brought her with me. And with her help, I learned to use and appreciate computers. The classes I teach now have more technology-based projects than other classes in our school.

My daughter not only taught me how to use a computer, she also changed my life and the lives of my students. She's my favorite teacher.

Wired Students

Like my daughter, most of our students enter middle school with computer experience. Eighty percent of my students have computers in their homes. Not all are Internet-connected, but parents often take their children to the library to do Net research. And many parents have access to the Internet and E-mail at work.

Anyone who works in our building in any capacity has an E-mail account.

Despite their level of computer experience, every student takes a self-paced, six-week keyboarding course in seventh grade. The course teaches a word processing program, ClarisWorks, to all students, and it gives those who already know keyboarding the opportunity to further develop their skills.

Computers and Eighth Grade English

New Routes to Old Goals

There's a reassuring constancy to the goals in eighth grade English.

Regardless of what social and economic changes sweep our world, students will always need to read skillfully, write clearly, and think critically. Technology doesn't change these goals. It simply changes the way we approach them. Computers offer students new pathways—more exciting, "traveler-friendly" routes—to the goals that I've always set for my eighth grade English classes.

Susan Eloise Hinton's novel, *The Outsiders*, has been part of my curriculum for years.

With computer-enhanced instruction, I see faster progress toward reading, writing, and critical thinking skills.

And I've always asked students to choose one of the book's main characters, then create a scrapbook based on events in the life of that character that didn't occur in the book. My aim is to have students "get inside" the character and understand his or her unique viewpoint.

The Net Works!
The electronic world at their disposal enables my students to do much more ambitious projects than they could before. They have access, through the Internet, to hundreds of *Outsider* Web sites, so there's more material to fire their imaginations. These sites also give my students the opportunity to learn how other students around the country understand the characters and events in the novel. The result is students who are more highly motivated and more focused.

My students' scrapbooks, created with the PowerPoint presentation program, are more elaborate and sophisticated than anything they could produce without electronic "cutting and pasting." But more important, I find that visiting Web sites really helps students get into the novel. They're exposed to many more thought-provoking views, most of them put forth by their peers. The Net creates a community of learners. In effect, my students take part in a nationwide seminar.

Computers give a new dimension to the projects I assign. The upshot is better learning by more motivated students. With computer-enhanced instruction, I see faster progress toward the reading, writing, and critical thinking skills I expect my eighth graders to develop. The same thing happens with other old projects that I give a new-tech twist.

Mini-Mystery Home Page
For years, my students, working in pairs, have written 300- to 500-word mini-mysteries they challenge readers to solve. The

goal of this popular exercise is to develop good writing skills. Computers move students toward this goal by facilitating the editing and rewriting processes. It's just easier to correct grammar, delete mistakes, rearrange paragraphs, and fiddle with syntax when the tool bar and all its functions are never more than a mouse click away. Correcting and re-correcting a text is a lot simpler when you're dealing with light on a screen rather than ink on a page.

Because computers bring so much ease to the editing process, my students understand that *any* mistake in something they publish on the Web is inexcusable. I think this attitude—that grammatical and syntactical

Computer Usage Test

True or False   *One hundred percent is required before a user's permit will be issued.*

T○ F○ 1. E-mail is not guaranteed to be private and others may be able to read it.

T○ F○ 2. School rules regarding harassment do not apply to E-mail.

T○ F○ 3. Swearing, vulgarities, or inappropriate words will result in the user losing computer privileges.

T○ F○ 4. Messages relating to, or in support of, illegal activities will result in the person's removal from computer usage.

T○ F○ 5. It's OK to read X-rated materials on the Web, as long as it's not during class time.

T○ F○ 6. Vandalism, abuse, or theft of the equipment will result in the loss of computer privileges for the rest of the school year, or longer if circumstances warrant.

T○ F○ 7. I can add programs to the machines or take programs off.

T○ F○ 8. I may use someone else's E-mail disk if I have his/her permission.

T○ F○ 9. Taking or destroying someone's disk will result in the loss of computer privileges.

T○ F○ 10. I can print materials without prior permission.

T○ F○ 11. I don't have to follow school policy if my parents give me permission to use any Web resources on a school computer.

T○ F○ 12. It is OK to give strangers my home address or phone number on E-mail or the Web.

T○ F○ 13. It's OK to teach other students how to hack.

T○ F○ 14. Flaming is OK if it's sent to friends.

T○ F○ 15. E-mail that harasses or threatens someone should be reported to the teacher.

errors are never to be tolerated—carries over to their work even when they're not using

> *The knowledge that they're writing for the whole wired world seems to make students take greater pride in their work.*

computers. And it makes them better writers.

The district media specialist and I teach the students how to set up a Web site with the ClarisWorks Home Page program. We teach them how to use the software to create links, choose fonts, download graphics, and import animated images. After I give the students guidelines telling them what elements they must include to be published on the Internet, they work at their own pace to create a Mini-Mystery Web page that combines lucid writing with inviting graphics.

Global Recognition

Our Mini-Mystery Web site is becoming increasingly popular, garnering more than 1,000 hits a month (http://www.isd77.k12.mn.us/schools/dakota/mystery/contents.html). Over a two-year period, 31,000 people have visited us. I've learned from E-mail messages that our site is a favorite for those who are learning English. The vocabulary is the right level, and readers have to complete interactive exercises in order to solve the mystery, so they're entertained while learning the language. Our reach is international: We have readers not just from every part of the United States, but from Bosnia and Japan as well!

Needless to say, this global impact has done wonders to pump up the confidence and enthusiasm of my eighth grade writers. The knowledge that they're writing for the whole wired world seems to make students take greater pride in their work. They're more conscientious. When they see sloppy writing on the web, they don't think it's cool. And they realize how much work they must do to avoid being embarrassed themselves.

Other Class Projects

The 5,000- to 6,000-word student autobiography is another one of my standard assignments that has been enhanced by technology. I've taught the unit for some 20 years because writing about themselves helps students overcome their fear of writing.

This unit also helps students expand their understanding of computer technology. Students use the software called Reunion to construct their family trees. They become proficient with scanning technology and digital cameras so they can incorporate family photos into their autobiographies. The use of graphics software enables them to further personalize their work.

The concept of tailoring your writing to a specific audience is of primary importance in this unit. Students know that the autobiographies are for their families. And they want a first-rate product. The quality of the documents that my students produce would not be possible without computer technology. Parents appreciate the professionalism of the final product. They're proud to see their family history presented in such a classy format.

Dakota Conflict Web Site

Mankato, unfortunately, is probably best known for being the site of the largest mass hanging in the United States. In 1862, the U.S. Cavalry hung 38 Native Americans who had taken part in an uprising that became known as the Dakota Conflict. This was the first of the Dakota prairie wars that ended in the massacre at Wounded Knee in South Dakota. It also led to the forcible removal of all Native Americans from southern Minnesota. For nearly 100 years, the Dakota Conflict stood as a barrier to communication between white people and Native Americans in central Minnesota.

In 1958, a spiritual and tribal leader of the Dakotas and a white Mankato businessman became friends and decided to begin the process of reconciliation. It's a continuing process that includes an annual powwow and ceremonies honoring the reconciliation. The naming of our school, which pays tribute to the Dakota nation, was also part of the healing process. The opening of the school featured a tribal elder's blessing and a performance by Dakota dancers.

CyberFair Contest

Early in the 1998-99 school year, I took one of my classes on a field trip related to the conflict. We visited museums, cemeteries, and other nearby sites. When I

> *The quality of the documents that my students produce would not be possible without computer technology.*

heard about the Global Schoolhouse CyberFair (http://www.globalschoolhouse.org) for student-created Web sites, I thought the Dakota Conflict and the reconciliation effort that followed would make ideal subject matter for a Web site we could submit to the CyberFair's historical landmark category.

The only problem—and it was a big one—was the March 31 deadline!

We were just completing the month-long autobiography project. On March 1, at the moment my students could finally take a deep breath and call this project a done deal, I gave them a choice: Work like crazy to create a Web site for the international CyberFair contest, or work on the site at a more deliberate pace and skip the contest until the next year. I told them that entering the CyberFair contest would make sense only if their commitment

We decided to work like crazy to create a Web site for the international CyberFair contest.

was strong. I made it plain that a "go for it" vote by a simple majority wouldn't be enough of a buy-in. We needed solidarity. After a discussion of pros and cons, more than 85 percent of the class voted to enter the contest.

And We Were Off!

We went to a Native American community about a hour from Mankato to interview tribal historians of the Dakota tribe. Students hit the Net, cemeteries, museums, and—yes—books.

Because so much had to be done so quickly, students assumed key managerial responsibilities. Nick, for example, had a study hall every day, and he became the scanner for tons of pictures and historical documents. He was our guru in that area. So if somebody asked, "Where's my picture of Henry Sibley?" Nick could say, "I've got it here on Disc 6." We called Nick the "Scan Man."

Students worked in teams to create Web pages. Linking these pages together in at least a semi-logical fashion became the class's most imposing challenge. In order to build a Web site, you need architects. And the architects need a site map—the rough equivalent of a blueprint.

Web architecture is rough going. When you have 50 different pages from 15 different teams of students, and when all pages must link in a manner that is helpful to the user of the Web site, your first map of the site will probably be of help only to people interested in becoming lost.

The students persevered.

Because of the suddenness of our decision to enter the CyberFair, we had no lab time scheduled to build our Web site. This meant everything had to be done outside of normal school hours. One Saturday, I had 14 kids spending all day in the lab. And we were there until six o'clock every night after school. The architects hung in there. The Web site got built.

On March 31, our D-Day, we were still proofing copy and double-checking the links on our Web site (http://www.isd77.k12.mn.us/schools/dakota/conflict/history.html). At 10:39 p.m., we officially entered the CyberFair competition. Whew!

A few weeks later, my students and I were delighted to learn that our Dakota Conflict site was one of five finalists in the historical landmark category. Then, in May, word came that we had won the grand prize in this category!

We were thrilled! And we were honored. But what matters most to all of us is that we're letting a worldwide audience know that the story of the Dakota Conflict did not end with that terrible violence in 1862. The reconciliation effort makes it a continuing, contemporary story. Because of the Internet, computer technology, and a group of dedicated eighth grade English students, Mankato's story will be known beyond Mankato. The story we told on the Web is the story of forgiveness and healing and understanding. It is the story of Mankato's past and of our future.

Internet Safety

Although middle school students have a strong sense of right and wrong, they often need to work on developing good judgment and a sense of responsibility. Our Internet policy, because it makes the consequences of poor choices so clear, helps students develop these virtues.

Each year, we mail copies of the school district's Internet Guidelines to students' parents or guardians. Parents must sign a document stating that they have read and discussed the Guidelines with their child. The student must also sign the same document and return it to the school before he or she can obtain computer privileges.

Media specialists and classroom teachers discuss the school's computer use policy with students. Students are required to pass a 15-point, true/false Computer Usage Test. They must score 100 percent to gain computer privileges. The test covers the district's Internet Guidelines and appropriate computer use. We issue a User Permit to a student only after he or she has successfully completed the Computer Usage Test. The User's Permit is signed by a teacher, the school's Media Specialist, and the student. Students must display the User's Permit at all times when using school computers.

Personal Responsibility

I am firmly against "blocking" software and "net nanny" mechanisms—for several reasons.

First, there's the cost. Any money spent on these programs is money you won't have for computer hardware and software. Second, even though many of the new censoring programs are very sophisticated, old or "cheap" programs usually don't think. They just block out words. Third, these blocking programs give parents and teachers alike a false sense of security: Hackers can break through the system of some of the older or cheaper programs. Finally, and this is my

I am firmly against "blocking" software and "net nanny" mechanisms.

strongest reason for opposing these mechanisms, I want to put my confidence in personal responsibility, not in a mechanical policing device.

In the long run, our students will be best served if we help them develop the good sense—and the good strong sense of responsibility—they will need to make sensible decisions and intelligent choices throughout their lives. We do them no favor if we set up a system that offers them no opportunity to practice personal responsibility.

Our students know they have to take responsibility for not abusing the system. If they don't follow the rules, they'll lose their computer privileges. The first year, we took our first student off within three hours of giving him his E-mail address. Because we've made the rules plain and made them tough, we've seen a decrease in abuse over the years. That first year, we had 11 students off computers for the whole year. This year, we had only one.

We do put a block on chatlines. Our school also has a system that allows us to see where everyone is on the computers. Students are not constantly monitored, but we check on them when we have reason to be concerned. In a way, this check-up is like a locker search that is conducted if we have probable cause.

Our students want the privilege of using technology. And they know there will be penalties if they abuse the privilege. This is not a complex system. And it's not perfect. But I know of none that is better.

Future Plans

One of my future goals is for my students to create more Web sites like the Dakota Conflict site. An important part of what my students have learned is that technology offers them a way to serve their community. The lesson I've learned is that I need to rely more on the talents of my students.

Students Are Technology Resources

My students are a wonderful technology resource. During the construction of the Dakota Conflict Web site, I discovered that one of my students had really mastered the program, MacPaint. So I had him teach the teams who thought they could use the MacPaint graphics program on their section of the Web site. I saw first-hand how effectively a knowledgeable student can teach the rest of the class.

Down the road, I plan to utilize the savvy kids in my class who excel in special areas. Some of them like Web Painter. Some of them know great sites for graphics. Others know Java Script, Avid Camera, and Adobe programs. And others have learned just by spending hours in front of the computer and poking around. These kids never read directions. They just get into a program and figure it out!

Gender Balance

I also intend to remain vigilant about avoiding gender bias and ensuring gender balance in technology. It would be tragic if technology came to be thought of as a "guy thing." Our society has enough stereotypes. We need to take care not to create more.

When I assign teams to be responsible for various parts of a Web site, I make sure that at least half of the team leaders are girls. And I like the fact that both media specialists I work with are female. When we're together, teaching the tricks of the tech trade, students see three females demonstrating their technological expertise. I think that sight delivers a valuable message—to young men as much as to young women.

Technology and the Mission of Public Schools

I believe that by integrating technology throughout a public school curriculum, Dakota Meadows Middle School has delivered powerful a message. We've made it our mission to ensure that Dakota Meadows graduates, whatever their parents' income level, will be as proficient with computers and as comfortable on the Internet as the graduates of private schools and the children of affluence. By making sure our students are at home in the information society and prepared for participation in a high-tech global village, we are advancing a primary goal of public education and making good on a precious promise of our democracy—equality of opportunity.

Teaching with Technology Reproducible 6.1

District Guidelines for Student Use of Internet Accounts

All Internet users are expected to abide by the generally accepted rules of computer and network etiquette. The following guidelines are the minimum taught to all district students:

1. Be polite. Do not get abusive in E-mail messages to others. School rules regarding harassment apply to electronic communication.

2. Use appropriate language. Do not swear, use vulgarities, or any other inappropriate language.

3. Do not reveal your personal address or the phone numbers of students or colleagues to unknown Internet users.

4. Be aware that E-mail is not guaranteed to be private. People who operate the system do have access to mail if there is probable cause to see it. Messages relating to or in support of illegal activities will be reported to the authorities.

5. There are some unacceptable uses of the networks. These include, but are not limited to:

    - Using the network for any illegal activity, including violation of copyright or other laws.
    - Using the network in ways that violate school policies and behavior standards.
    - Using the network for financial or commercial gain.
    - Degrading or disrupting equipment or system performance.
    - Invading the privacy of other individuals by accessing and/or vandalizing their computerized data.
    - Wasting technology resources, including bandwidth, file space, and printers.
    - Gaining unauthorized access to resources or entities.
    - Using an account owned by another user, with or without his/her permission.
    - Posting personal communications without the author's consent.

6. Any items produced by the students will not be posted to the Internet without their permission. If permission is granted, items will be considered fair use and available to the public.

Reader Reflections

Insights: _____

_____

_____

_____

_____

_____

_____

Actions for Our School, District, or Association To Consider: _____

_____

_____

_____

_____

_____

_____

Teacher Review

Beyond Textbooks: Hands-On Learning
USING THE PRESENT TO TEACH THE PAST

When I was a student, I had to interview my mother as a project for one of my classes. My mother, who grew up in Arkansas in the 1950s, recounted her experiences with bomb shelters, integration, and hiding under her desk in nuclear war drills. I had read about these events, but when I pictured my mother, as a little girl, witnessing these things, they finally became vivid and real. It was the kind of experience we should try to provide for our students more often. That's why I was so impressed with the article "Using the Present to Teach the Past."

In her classes, Carol Steele makes history real by connecting it to living people. The unit involves students in talking to senior citizens at a nearby apartment complex and creating either a historical fiction or nonfiction account of what they learned in the interviews. It started off simply, with one senior citizen's visit to Steele's class, and ended with the students conducting interviews for broadcast on a local public-access channel. This lesson is uncomplicated enough that it could be tried by a beginning teacher, but it's got a lot going for it, both in hard content and in intangibles like breaking down generational barriers while increasing community support for the school. Steele prepped her students by discussing stereotypes of the elderly in English class. She also had the students share their oral history projects with the seniors when they were finished.

The nice thing about this kind of lesson is that it involves students in a real-life activity, one that they will instantly recognize as being important, both for the community and for their own personal growth. When they have something they can sink their teeth into, students become motivated. When they are motivated to do well, they will learn. Sometimes the most turned-off teenagers just need work that feels more like an accomplishment than an assignment.

Ron Stanley
English Teacher
Mountain View Alternative High School
Arlington, Virginia

USING THE PRESENT TO TEACH THE PAST

A textbook could never match the knowledge these high school students gained from oral histories with elderly neighbors.

7

"Every time an old person dies, it's like a library burning down." This quote has always resonated with me. Two years ago it weighed on my mind as I gazed out of the window of my second-floor classroom. Just up the hill, past the tennis courts, sits an eleven-story senior citizens' building called The Grandview Apartments.

As a history teacher, I had formulated two goals in regard to a more authentic approach to teaching history. One of my goals was to help students realize that not all history is learned from textbooks. Real people experience these things, and soon what you've experienced will become someone else's history.

My other goal was to overcome the categorization, divisions, and stereotypes that exist between students and elderly people. I wanted my students to see that the older generation has something to offer as well. Elderly people are not only a source of history, but nice people who should not be written off or avoided.

It's important in teaching American history to get to the present, or at least the students' lifetime. I've often noticed that teachers run out of time just as the curriculum reaches World War II or the Korean War. I wanted my students to get exposed to the whole span of history. And I felt that they should acquire that knowledge from people who had experienced it, not just from books.

I also wanted my students to perform some sort of service as part of their learning during the year. I'd heard of the Foxfire series and had listened to a day-long presentation on implementing service learning, but both seemed complicated

CAROL STEELE

English and History Teacher

Union High School

Grand Rapids, Michigan

THE ULTIMATE BEGINNER'S GUIDE   89

and beyond what I could visualize. I knew I would have to choose something small, something I could reasonably hope to do.

Union High

I've been teaching at Union High School, an urban high school with about 1,400 students in Grand Rapids, Michigan, for the last four years. Grand Rapids is the second largest city in Michigan. It has a diversified economy that usually remains fairly stable even during downturns.

Because Union High is the county bilingual center, we have several hundred students from sixteen nations this year, alongside a regular high school program. We are probably more diverse than any other school in western Michigan.

The area surrounding Union High is strongly blue-collar, with many elderly residents and pockets of suburbia.

It is a section of city that traditionally votes against increased public monies for schools even when the rest of the city votes yes. This is one reason most of our staff believe a closer relationship with the community would benefit the school.

The Elderly As a Resource

The Grandview Apartments is not a nursing home. It's a federally subsidized housing site for low-income adults. Most residents are retirees in their sixties, seventies, or eighties. A small number have physical handicaps, but most are actively involved in the scheduled activities at the apartments or in volunteer work in the community, or both.

In the spring of 1993, I called The Grandview's manager and told him I wanted to invite some seniors down to my classroom to talk about their memories of World War II. The manager agreed to post a notice on the bulletin board. While I only got one response, that response was spectacular. Mrs. Evelyn Stewart called to volunteer as a speaker while we were studying the 1940s.

When she came, Mrs. Stewart turned out to be a cozy-looking woman with glowing, shoulder-length white hair. She brought a bulging scrapbook that had been assembled by her deceased husband's mother during World War II. Mrs. Stewart also brought typed notes she had prepared for the speech and spent an hour regaling the class with real-life experiences. She even left the scrapbook with us for several weeks to let students have time to browse through it. Since she was a little nervous, Mrs. Stewart also brought an even older lady who sat silently in the back just to offer moral support.

Mrs. Stewart was twelve years old when

One of my goals was to help my students realize that not all history is learned from books.

Pearl Harbor was bombed by the Japanese in 1941. When she heard the news, she became fearful planes would appear overhead and drop bombs on her. She remembered the crowds of men driving to the recruiting station to sign up. Although she had been a witness to history, the students tended to ask her about things relevant to her own life experiences: Did you have dances back then? What was dating like? How did your husband propose?

As the school year began in the fall of 1993, I had volunteered for a new challenge in teaching. For the first time I was teaching a block of U.S. History and English to tenth graders whom I kept for two successive hours. I wanted to teach so that students would see how learning in the two areas was related.

After my positive experience with one resident of the Grandview, I thought perhaps I could recruit more seniors there and plan a unit on oral history. I decided to contact a district school administrator who coordinates programs for senior citizens. She provided the name of a contact person at the Grandview—Mrs. Ruth Kuntz, the woman who puts together the residents' newsletter.

I contacted Mrs. Kuntz and she agreed to help. Together we selected days and times for the students to meet with the senior citizens in the community room at the complex. Mrs. Kuntz agreed to find ten interested seniors to work with each of my two blocked classes. Since the building is close enough to walk to even in cold weather, logistics were simple. All I needed were permission slips from parents so that students could leave the school grounds.

I decided three visits on successive weeks would be long enough to form a relationship, and short enough that if I fell on my face and the unit failed, none of us would be committed for a really long period. I developed a long list of questions for each visit, but told students they were free to follow their own conversations. The questions were a backup, in case it was hard for students to think of what to ask.

Hot Chocolate to the Rescue

The students were not enthusiastic when they first heard about the plan. There was some groaning and a number of cool stares as I explained. We explored stereotypes of elderly people in our English classes by brainstorming words and listing them on the blackboard; the list was weighted heavily toward negatives.

Still, on the appointed day, we trudged up the hill in absolutely frigid temperatures and cautiously entered the apartment building. I had divided the students into groups of three or four so that each small group could meet one of the ten senior citizens I hoped would be waiting for us there. When we got inside, students flocked over to the urn of hot chocolate their

Authentic History Lessons Pay Off

Some of my students entered a National History Day competition. Two of my groups won in the media division. One group had a ten-minute video on Prohibition. They are going to the state finals. As part of their presentation, they dress up in 1920s style and recite facts about the decade and a half when alcoholic beverages were illegal in the United States.

hosts had ready for them and began to warm up to the idea of interviewing.

Some senior citizens arrived late, but Mrs. Kuntz finally rounded them all up, including Mrs. Stewart, whom I'd met the previous year. The students spent about seventy-five minutes talking as I circulated among groups; then we went back to the classroom in time for the bell that ends second hour. My afternoon block went on a different day and met with another group of ten adults whom they interviewed.

The schedule was the same for each of the three interview days. The students' attitudes quickly changed, progressing from negative or neutral to positive or enthusiastic. They got to know individual elders and began to enjoy themselves.

The students got a lot more social history and daily life history than they would've gotten from books. Through the interviews, they saw how life affected people forty or fifty years ago. They also changed attitudes. At first, getting them to go to Grandview was like getting them to go for oral surgery. But by the second or third visit, students would say things like "Our lady is so cute!" or "I can't wait to get over there!"

Because of illness or schedule conflicts, not all the seniors could keep coming. Sometimes Mrs. Kuntz found replacements; other times we put more students with the available adults. In some cases the groups began to bond; seniors greeted us at the door with "Where are my boys?" or "Aren't Tiffany and Kara here?" Even in other groups a level of cordiality was soon reached.

By week two, the students were admitting that their experience at the Grandview was not at all what they had expected. They found the senior citizens both interesting and likable. On the last of our scheduled three meetings, right after our requested rendition of the school fight song (demanded by senior citizen alumnae of Union), I found myself promising that we would come back after we had done our oral history reports so that the senior citizens could see the work the students produced.

Oral History Writing Assignments

Back in the classroom, students could choose to do either a report or a piece of historical fiction based on the stories they'd heard. Illustrations were required. The work was generally good and about equally divided between the two approaches. Unfortunately, students don't get enough experience writing to get better at it. Even worse, their writing assignments often

The students got a lot more social history and daily life history than they would've gotten from books.

consist of regurgitating material. But here they were writing about things that felt real, in contrast to ordinary writing assignments.

During one of our visits, Mrs. Stewart heard the students talking about plays they were writing for me in English class and proposed an idea. Could our students perform a play for the seniors at one of their monthly "theatre luncheons"? (These consisted of a short play and a big potluck meal.) I agreed that we would try. Mrs. Stewart suggested that the students could read and share their history reports during the same session.

Lights, Camera, Interview!

As my students and I prepared, I got another call from Mrs. Stewart. Now the senior citizens were wondering if our students could participate in an intergenerational TV show. The Retired Senior Volunteer Program produces and broadcasts a weekly show on the public-access channel in Grand Rapids. I agreed to help work it out.

First, three students attended the open house scheduled at the TV station. Then we talked over the opportunity in class and the students expressed interest. We brainstormed long lists of questions we could ask of senior citizens on the first broadcast and questions we'd like them to ask us during the second one.

Intriguing questions arose during this planning. For instance, could we ask elderly people about euthanasia and assisted suicide? On the one hand, it would be enlightening to find out their views; on the other, such questions might be considered indelicate. This issue was resolved by including the question and asking the producer, Sarah Lowe, herself a senior citizen, to screen the questions and delete any she deemed inappropriate.

On the appointed afternoon, I used the school station wagon to transport eight students to Channel 23 in Wyoming, Michigan, a suburb about twenty minutes from our school. The two half-hour TV shows were taped back-to-back. We were there nearly three hours.

Naturally, the students were nervous at first, but after a few minutes in the lounge getting introduced to senior citizens and the pop machine, they began to loosen up. They also got a quick tour

The Foxfire Series

The Foxfire learning concept is based on four precepts:
1. Learn by doing.
2. Use the community as a classroom.
3. Explore the local culture.
4. Produce a project.

of the equipment and the control room before taping began. It took about half an hour just to get everyone seated and get the lights, equipment, microphones, and sound levels prepared for taping. Each student's first response in the panel discussions was a bit stiff, but I was surprised at how quickly they forgot the cameras and focused on the interchanges between seniors and students. They covered a wide range of subjects as the cameras rolled.

The tapes were scheduled for broadcasting during our spring vacation and the following week. But Mrs. Stewart, who always seems to think of everything, arranged for extra copies to be dubbed for the school and for any student who provided a tape. After spring vacation, we took time in class to view both programs. There was some ribbing of students whose mannerisms were captured by the camera but also a strong interest among all members of the two classes, whether they had appeared on tape or not.

The senior citizens were delighted by their intergenerational programs, so delighted that they requested another such series for next fall.

Our last activity with the residents of the Grandview was the theater luncheon put on by each of the two groups. The morning class went in late April and the afternoon group in early May. Each group presented a play or skit, then read some of the oral history projects, and left the originals with the senior citizens who had inspired them. The senior citizens brought casseroles and salads and all sorts of other goodies. The students brought desserts. The spread of food was a feast, and the camaraderie between young and old was wonderful.

The groups began to bond. Seniors greeted us at the door with "Where are my boys?" or "Aren't Tiffany and Kara here?"

Looking back, I'm surprised at how simple the project was. I really expected it to take more time and effort on my part than it did. The senior citizens were energetic and eager to help and easily fitted our visits into existing systems. For instance, they recruited other Grandview residents to be interviewed through their building newsletter and later simply plugged us into the TV series.

Assessing Growth

The change in the students was quite noticeable. They were reluctant to go at first, but once they tried it they liked it. Most set aside their prejudices, finding the senior citizens likable and not at all depressing. Most also recommended that I repeat the project next year because it was so interesting and different. Feedback from parents and administration was quite positive.

The Authentic Materials Approach

What's unique about authentic learning as applied to my students? It's interactive, for one thing. A student asks a question, gets the answer, and then can ask another question. Or the student can take a new tack, for example, asking about the meaning of a particular word. A book may have a paragraph on the whaling industry, but with an authentic-learning approach you're able to talk to someone who spent years involved first-hand with something like that, and you're sure to get more than a paragraph's worth of memorable information.

Probably the best testimonial to the success of our authentic-learning experience came from the senior citizens themselves. They were absolutely delighted by every visit by the young people. They had hot chocolate waiting in the winter and punch in the spring. The kids basked in their warmth and formed new opinions of aging in America. From a political point of view, maybe increased contact with the young will create a greater willingness among retirees in our area to support school-funding issues.

Now that I know how easily we can work with the seniors who live just up the hill, I'm sure I'll include interactions between them and my students every year. I will definitely do an oral history project next year, but something tells me we'll dream up new variations and additions as we go along.

Beyond Textbooks Reproducible 7.1

Oral History Report Options

(These options were given to students writing oral history reports on their interviews with elderly residents at Grandview Apartments.)

You may choose one of the options below as you prepare your report based on the interviews at Grandview apartments. Whichever one you choose, be sure to include credits or acknowledgments to the people who provide you with information.

A. Historical Fiction - You may take the information you gathered and create a story from it, like an illustrated children's story book. You might re-combine the facts from one person or use facts from several people as long as the story remains a truthful representation of the era you are describing (the result might be like Laura Ingalls Wilder's books or entirely your own approach).

B. Nonfiction Account - Here you must report the information with complete accuracy, checking facts with other sources such as encyclopedias when you need to verify something. In this approach, you will quote individuals who provide unusual anecdotes or personal outlooks that are used in your report.

*Beyond Textbooks
Reproducible 7.2a*

Suggested Questions for Oral History Interviews

As we travel to Grandview, remember that you represent Union High School. Please be courteous. Take the first few minutes of your time to introduce the members of the group briefly. You may ask any appropriate question to find out about your elder's early life. The questions below are suggestions you may turn to if you run out of ideas:

1. Where did you grow up? What was it like there?
2. Tell us about the members of your family.
3. What are your earliest memories?
4. Describe a typical school day in your elementary school.
5. What did you study?
6. What was the school room like?
7. How did you get to school?
8. What games and activities did you take part in as a child?
9. Describe your chores and family responsibilities while growing up.
10. Describe your family's holiday observances: Fourth of July, Christmas, Easter or Passover, Thanksgiving, etc.
11. Were birthdays celebrated in your home?
12. Describe your parents' jobs and family responsibilities.

(Continued)

THE ULTIMATE BEGINNER'S GUIDE

Beyond Textbooks Reproducible 7.2b

Suggested Questions for Oral History Interviews
(Continued)

13. Did your family can foods, butcher meat, make soap, or do other tasks that aren't usually done at home today? Tell us how.

14. What religious customs, if any, did your family have?

15. What was your normal clothing as a child or teenager?

16. When and how did you get new clothes or shoes?

17. What was teenage social life like when you were in high school?

18. What behavior was required or expected that is different from today? How was politeness defined then?

19. What were your favorite activities or places to go?

20. What was your house like? How did you get around?

21. Tell us about your first job.

22. Describe some historic events you recall. (Pearl Harbor, Great Depression, Korean Conflict)

23. If you married, how did you meet your spouse? What was your wedding like?

24. What relatives were important to you or close to you? Can you tell us some of the stories they told you or things you did together?

25. What about your own children or nieces, nephews, etc. How did you go about raising them?

26. What advice would you give to modern teens?

Reader Reflections

Insights: _____

_____

_____

_____

_____

Actions for Our School (District) To Consider: _____

_____

_____

_____

_____

_____

_____

Teacher Review

Peer Support: Teachers Mentoring Teachers

SHARING THE WEALTH

As a first-year teacher, I was instructed to pick a subject to focus on for the year and perfect it. How did I know what to choose? A subject in which I had some mastery or one in which my knowledge was limited? I was at a loss as to what my focus would be until a veteran third grade teacher assumed the role of mentor. We met and discussed the third grade curriculum and chose reading instruction as my focus. We now talk informally each day and meet formally every one-to-two weeks. As "Sharing the Wealth" reveals, I found that it's important to set up a reciprocal relationship with a mentor because you are presented with a new challenge each day.

Outlined in the story are six points of advice for forming a successful mentor-mentee relationship. For instance, I've always wondered where teachers get their materials, classroom books, lesson ideas, etc. Now I know: They share! I believe that one's colleagues are a new teacher's most valuable resource, and they are often willing to help.

The value of a mentor-mentee relationship is immeasurable. I've benefited greatly from preparing questions or concerns before an "official" meeting with my mentor, and I feel more confident in my opinion when I can share ideas. Just like the teachers in "Sharing the Wealth," I've learned so much from my colleague, mentor, and friend across the hall this year. I would recommend "Sharing the Wealth" to any new teacher. I only wish I had read it before I started teaching!

Jessica Price
3rd Grade Teacher
West District Elementary School
Farmington, Connecticut

SHARING THE WEALTH

Would a wealth of experience retire with veteran teachers? The local association creates a mentoring program to help its newest members.

8

Linda was late for lunch. When she finally arrived, she told us she couldn't believe what she had just been told. It was the middle of the school year and two of our new teachers, Emily and Jill, were without curriculum guides. They were floundering and they didn't know where to turn. How could this have happened?

Actually, such a mix-up was quite easy. Budget constraints had eliminated the department heads who normally would have issued the guides. Veteran teachers could have stepped in, but it had been so long since new teachers were in the building that veterans forgot what it was like. The safety net enjoyed by new teachers so many years ago was gone.

Fortunately, Linda Breen, a ninth grade English teacher who has taught in the district for 25 years, was able to provide the curriculum guides, make suggestions, and give Emily and Jill the support they needed and

**ELLIE HANLON
JENNIFER CURTIS
LORI GOODINE**

Weymouth, Massachusetts

deserved. This was a rude awakening. The first year of teaching is stressful enough, but to have new teachers isolated and alone was unthinkable. If this was happening here, then it was surely happening in other schools in our district.

Weymouth, with a population of 54,000, is the third-largest town in the state of Massachusetts. A former seaside resort, Weymouth is a residential middle-income community that lies 17 miles south of Boston. In recent years, Weymouth's student population has grown more diverse, and the school system now serves a

THE ULTIMATE BEGINNER'S GUIDE 101

small but growing percentage of ESL students, many from Brazil, Vietnam, and Cambodia. Weymouth currently has a student population of approximately 6,700.

Since the early 1980s, a continuing round of budget cuts and declining student enrollment has reduced the number of available schools in Weymouth by half. Less money and fewer students meant that, up until five years ago, virtually no new teachers were hired by the district. Then an infusion of new state aid

There was no vehicle in place to pass on our methods to the next generation of teachers.

under the Education Reform Act, and increased retirements, started bringing many new teachers into our district. Like Emily and Jill, these newcomers often needed a helping hand. The Weymouth Teachers Association (WTA) realized that we needed to make sure our newest colleagues would have somewhere to turn for guidance and support during their first year of teaching. We discovered that many of the simple things we take for granted were stumbling blocks for our new teachers:

- Where do you go for supplies?
- How do you call in sick?
- What is a personal day? How do you apply for one?
- How do you apply for a conference day?
- When are special reports due?
- What can I expect at Back-to-School Night?

These and other details needed to be explained, but we also wanted to give new and veteran staff the opportunity to share different teaching ideas and instructional strategies with one another.

Passing the Torch

Unfortunately, teaching schedules allowed no time for any of the teachers to meet, talk, or exchange ideas during the course of the school day. And family commitments, course work, and extracurricular activities made after-school meetings difficult. We had so much to share with one another and no time to meet. Most of the staff would be retiring within the next ten years. Sadly, there was no vehicle in place to pass on our tried-and-true methods of presenting materials or managing classrooms to the next generation of teachers. Our special lessons, projects, and units would retire with us.

What were we going to do? Was it really necessary for the next generation to rediscover the special projects that we had used so successfully? How could we share the best of our teaching with our newest colleagues?

The Association Steps In
—Ellie Hanlon

I've been president of the WTA since 1993. In 1995, the WTA decided to create a Pre-K–12 peer mentoring program that would provide a support system for our newest members and give veteran teachers the opportunity to share their knowledge and experience with one another as well as their mentees.

WTA's Sharing the Wealth Mentoring Program would consist of three components:

1) Mentors who worked in the same building as the new teachers would provide daily one-on-one contact and support;

2) Theme mentors (teachers with special expertise in certain content areas) would be available on an as-needed basis; and

3) Monthly townwide sessions would be held off school grounds and would cover topics of common concern to all teachers.

Starting the Program

Recruiting Mentors

During the months of July and August, I sent out a newsletter asking for volunteer mentors for our program. The response was tremendous. Throughout the summer, teachers called the WTA office to sign on as volunteers. Once school started in September, I sent a follow-up letter describing the program to all of our members. We asked them to approach new teachers in their building during the first week of school and offer to be a mentor.

Our veteran teachers were so eager to help their new colleagues, we ended up with more mentors than newcomers—50 volunteers for a total of 20 new teachers. Volunteers in schools where there were no new teachers were put on a waiting list. (These volunteers attended the meetings we held throughout the school year so they would be prepared for next year.) Volunteers in schools with a limited number of new teachers sometimes ended up sharing a mentee. Several guidance counselors also served as additional mentors for beginning teachers.

Advice from Mentees

1. Allow both parties to choose their partners.
2. Allow the people working together time alone to voice opinions and share ideas.
3. Incorporate sessions that discuss school policy or information that veteran teachers sometimes take for granted.
4. Share classroom educational materials and resources. Newer teachers have not had the time to acquire an abundance of worthwhile materials.
5. Be patient. Change seldom occurs on the first try and it does not happen overnight.
6. Recognize the value of your current teaching staff, regardless of age or years of experience.

Theme Mentors

We use theme mentors as well as individual mentors in an effort to include more of our teachers. Theme mentors serve as resource people in their buildings for specific subjects. For example, at the junior high school, two computer science teachers provide help and assistance to teachers in the MAC lab or in the IBM lab. Industrial technology teachers at both intermediate schools and the junior high school are available to advise their colleagues and to build sets for plays and concerts. At the high school, several of the English teachers serve as writing theme mentors for teachers in other disciplines. The process is informal—teachers are given the name of the theme mentor in their building, and anyone who needs help can call or drop by for advice.

Kick-Off Meeting

We decided to hold the kick-off meeting for our peer mentoring program on September 18. To prepare, I sent a letter to all the new teachers, welcoming them to the school system, outlining the mentoring program, and inviting them to our first "townwide" mentoring session.

All of our monthly townwide sessions, including the kick-off meeting, were held at a local restaurant called the Village Steakhouse. The kick-off meeting was an informal orientation session that lasted two hours. We described the program, assigned mentors to two teachers who didn't have one yet, and handed out a survey asking teachers what topics they wanted to cover during our meetings and what guest speakers they wanted to hear. In addition, Ron Suga, our UniServ Director, gave the teachers an overview of the WTA and the National Education Association.

I also prepared a guidebook for new teachers and distributed it at the kick-off meeting. The book includes important school dates, procedures for calling in sick, tips for dealing with difficult parents, suggestions for improving communications between home and school, school rules and regulations, and lots of other practical tips and useful information. It also includes all of the forms teachers need during the school year.

Townwide Sessions

The WTA continued to hold monthly townwide sessions off

We held monthly townwide sessions off school grounds where participants felt free to ask questions.

school grounds where participants felt free to ask questions and bring up concerns. The sessions brought together K–12 teachers from all over town to share ideas, strategies, and lessons. Often, the topics of these sessions were generated by the specific experiences of the mentors and mentees. Our most successful session was born from a difficult situation involving Linda and Kelly.

Linda and Kelly

A parent had requested a meeting with Kelly, a new junior high school science teacher, without giving a reason for her request. This was unusual, so Linda Breen, Kelly's mentor, offered to go to the meeting with her. The parent wasn't pleased that another teacher was going to sit in on the meeting, but Linda explained to the mother that as one of her daughter's teachers, she could add to the discussion of any problem that might exist. When the mother immediately launched into an attack on Kelly and her teaching methods, Kelly was dumbfounded. The mother's complaints had nothing to do with her own child, but rather with an alleged incident with another child in the class. The mother had decided that it was her duty to set this new, young teacher "straight."

Linda, an experienced teacher with a talent for conflict resolution, intervened and diffused a difficult situation for Kelly. Linda asked key questions and calmly clarified the situation. She reasoned with the parent and pointed out that the parent's reaction was based on secondhand misinformation. She reiterated that the incident had nothing to do with the parent's child. The parent calmed down and acknowledged that Linda was right.

While Kelly was grateful for Linda's ability to take charge of a hostile meeting, she was unsure of what would have happened if she had been alone. Her vulnerability in this situation alarmed her. She suggested that all new teachers would benefit from a session on how to handle difficult situations.

Everything You've Always Wanted To Know

In response to Kelly's suggestion, we developed a session called "Everything You've Always Wanted To Know but Were

All new teachers would benefit from a session on how to handle difficult situations.

Afraid To Ask." It turned out to be one of the best sessions we've ever had. Kelly started off the

> **Advice from Mentors**
>
> 1. Make sure the agenda for each meeting is relevant to the teachers.
> 2. Ask for input from the teachers. Hold meetings off school grounds. Make it clear that sensitive or confidential issues will not be repeated outside the meeting.
> 3. Inform administrators of your objectives so they don't think the meetings are merely gripe sessions.
> 4. The program leader should be upbeat, organized, a good facilitator, and empathic.
> 5. Invite guest speakers with new ideas who will motivate teachers and help foster creative thinking.
> 6. There are no clear-cut right or wrong approaches to solving a problem. All ideas and strategies are to be shared and celebrated.

meeting by sharing her incident. Kelly's recounting of her experience struck a nerve with her colleagues. One story led to another and then another, as teachers related similar incidents. We realized that teachers new to the profession were unsure of their rights and tentative about how to handle themselves in difficult situations. Ron Suga assured the new teachers that no one had the right to "attack" them. He told them that if they found themselves alone in a similar situation, they should calmly get the parent back on the topic. If this failed, they should politely suggest that the meeting be rescheduled for another time and a "mediator" included.

Ron also gave suggestions on how to work with principals and other administrators. He advised new teachers who did not yet have professional status to let experienced teachers run interference if a problem arose. What was supposed to be a two-hour meeting turned into three-plus hours as questions flew and teachers shared their concerns. The meeting was so successful, we had to schedule a second session, "Everything II," to make up for the overflow.

These sessions were invaluable for the WTA as well as the students. Because we have thirteen schools in our local and all of the officers are full-time teachers, our ability to visit different sites is seriously limited. The sessions let us know exactly what was going on in different schools. We realized that teachers needed to know more about their rights, the evaluation process, what to do if they disagreed with an evaluation, and how to handle conflict (whether it was with a student, a parent, a teacher or an administrator). The "Everything" sessions gave birth to three new sessions: "Teachers' Rights," "Evaluations," and "Conflict Resolution."

Working with ESL Students

Another workshop session was born of an issue that concerned new and veteran teachers alike—

the influx of non-English speaking students mainstreamed into the regular classroom. We were fortunate that Peg Fasino, our ESL teacher, was willing to conduct a workshop to address specific concerns in this area.

Peg spent the first 45 minutes of the meeting describing the background of some of the ESL students and how cultural mores influence their behavior. For instance, she explained to teachers that some of their Asian students would not look at them when answering a question because, in their culture, it's considered rude for children to look a teacher in the eye. She also explained that some of their Cambodian and Vietnamese students might have problems getting along because of the history of conflict between these two countries. Background information like this made a world of difference because it helped teachers understand what motivated their students' behavior.

Next, Peg talked about research results on ESL students and how to use this information in the classroom. She gave practical suggestions for dealing with the language barrier, giving teachers handouts and worksheets to use with their students.

Peg's tips and techniques for working with students with limited English proficiency were invaluable. Many of the teachers left feeling more self-confident because some of the strategies they were already using in their classrooms had been validated by an expert in the field. In addition, the teachers now knew Peg and felt comfortable calling on her for specific problems.

Holiday Lesson Exchange

Since sharing is the theme of our mentoring program, we decided to host a townwide lesson exchange for the holiday session. I put a bulletin in the newsletter and sent a "hot line" (a brief notice on neon-bright paper) to all the schools asking teachers for their best lesson plans. Teachers who were willing to share that special lesson plan with their townwide colleagues brought 25 copies of it with them to the holiday session. If they were unable to attend but wanted to participate, they sent the lesson plan to the WTA office and we made copies and brought them to the session. I organized the lesson plans by grade level

We decided to host a townwide lesson exchange for the holiday session.

and subject area and laid them out so teachers could take the ones they wanted.

The lesson exchange was a big hit. Teachers not only had the opportunity to see what others were doing in their subject area and grade level but were able to showcase their own outstanding lessons. Now we swap lessons every holiday season. Last year, in addition to the lesson exchange, I downloaded NEA's Works4Me Tips for Teachers, organized them by subject and grade level, and compiled a booklet to pass out to teachers.

The best thing about the mentoring program was the opportunity to nurture budding friendships.

Evaluating the First Year

Most of our workshop sessions were a direct response to particular problems raised by teachers. They were encouraged to call the WTA office with concerns or to talk to any of the mentors about topics they were interested in discussing.

The only real concern teachers expressed was not having enough time to meet during the day. When we discussed this issue with the administration, they arranged for teachers to have release time to observe each other's classes.

The evaluation passed out at our final session solicited critiques of the different workshops and suggestions for new topics and program procedures for the next year. One of the evaluation questions concerned the matching process between mentor and mentee. Teachers indicated that they liked the procedure we used: they preferred being approached personally rather than being assigned to someone. They also liked the fact that meetings were held off school grounds. It gave them a "safe haven" and a feeling of confidentiality.

For many teachers, the best thing about the mentoring program was the opportunity to nurture budding friendships and expand their horizons, a sentiment shared by Jennifer Curtis and Lori Goodine, two first-grade teachers at Ralph Talbot Elementary School.

Lori and Jennifer

Jennifer was excited but anxious about being a new first-grade teacher. She knew that first grade is a pivotal year because it's the year many children learn to read and write. Like many teachers, Jennifer was concerned about pacing her lessons and working her way through the entire curriculum by the end of the school year. She also needed answers to all the basic questions new teachers have: Where could she find supplies for her classroom? What was the proper way to fill out report cards for Talbot? How could she stop her students from jumping up to sharpen their pencils in the middle of a lesson?

Fortunately, Lori Goodine, a six-year teacher, taught first grade right across the hall from Jennifer. Lori's offer to become Jennifer's mentor was the beginning of a wonderful professional and personal relationship for both teachers. Lori guided Jennifer through the shoals of her first year at Talbot, providing practical tips for questions about eager pencil sharpeners (reward all students who sharpened their pencils during the first few minutes of class) and answering more fundamental questions about curriculum pacing. Together, Lori and Jennifer went over lesson plans, shared curriculum materials, created new lessons, and reviewed lessons that didn't go as planned. Jennifer's and Lori's students even did class projects together.

At one point in the school year, Jennifer became concerned that some of her students weren't absorbing the phonics lessons. No matter how many times Jennifer went over and over the vowel sounds, these students just weren't "getting it." Lori, who was certified in Project Read, a national reading program, suggested that Jennifer use hand puppets to teach the children phonics. The children were delighted, and when Jennifer opened a puppet's mouth and made it "talk," the students learned how to position their own mouths to make the same sounds. Jennifer, a certified Special Education teacher with a beautiful singing voice, also used songs to teach her students to read. She was excited when she started to see results—her students were transferring the skills they had learned in class and were reading on their own.

Lori and Jennifer talked informally every day, and they scheduled at least one meeting a week to sit down and go over lessons. Although the two teachers usually met in the morning before school started, they occasionally got together during their preparation periods or after school hours.

"It was a reciprocal relationship," says Lori. "We both learned a lot. We sought each other out daily for advice, support, or a comforting shoulder to cry on. One thing we rarely feel any more is the sense of isolation. The mentoring program was a catalyst for our networking and sharing. Its effects will be lifelong."

Teachers Are Agents of Change

The Sharing the Wealth Mentoring program is now three years old, and its success can be attributed to the fact that the participants shared a great deal more than lesson plans. Teachers are just beginning to realize that we are critical change agents and that we must support one another to create important and productive change within the schools. When we have a non-threatening and supportive forum, the stresses are diminished and we are able to develop a healthy perspective. Systemic changes in a school system will take on exciting new dimensions when teachers are relaxed, listened to, and a part of the change process.

Peer Support
Reproducible 8.1

Program Evaluation

This evaluation was given to mentors and mentees in the Share the Wealth program.

1. Assignment of mentors (which would you prefer?):
   a. Have a veteran teacher within the building approach the new teacher about mentoring.
   b. Have the Association assign a mentor prior to the opening day of school.
   c. Other
   _____
   _____

2. Townwide mentoring sessions (which would you prefer?):
   a. Schedule meetings once a month.
   b. Select topics and schedule and post meeting dates in September. The number of sessions would depend on the topics chosen.
   c. Other
   _____
   _____

3. Were the townwide sessions helpful? Which one(s) met your needs best?
   List topics you would like to see included.
   _____
   _____

4. Did having a mentor help you adjust to the Weymouth Public School System? How?
   _____
   _____

5. What can we do to make the program better?
   _____
   _____

Peer Support Reproducible 8.2

Sharing the Wealth Mentoring Calendar

At the beginning of the school year, we give teachers a calendar of townwide meetings that includes dates and topics. The schedule is flexible, allowing us to include or substitute topics teachers feel are important.

Wednesday, September 15	Kick-Off
Wednesday, October 9	Everything You've Always Wanted To Know but Were Afraid To Ask
Wednesday, November 13	Teacher Rights
Wednesday, December 11	Lesson Plans Swap Party
Wednesday, January 15	Teacher Evaluations
Wednesday, February 5	Conflict Resolution
Wednesday, March 12	Recertification/Ed Reform
Wednesday, April 9	Tips/Techniques for Working with ESL Students
Wednesday, May 14	End-of the-Year Forms
Wednesday, June 11	Evaluation Party

Reader Reflections

Insights: _____

_____

_____

_____

_____

_____

_____

Actions for Our School, District, or Association To Consider: _____

_____

_____

_____

_____

_____

_____

_____

Selected Resources

Books

Bercik, J. 1994. *Joining Forces to Guide the New Teacher.* National Book Co.

Bosch, K.A. and K.A. Kersey. 2000. *The First-Year Teacher: Teaching with Confidence.* Washington DC: National Education Association.

Clement, M.C. 1997. *Bright Ideas: A Pocket Mentor for Beginning Teachers.* Washington DC: National Education Association.

Cowles, M. and J. Aldridge. 1992. *Activity-Oriented Classrooms, K-3.* Washington DC: National Education Association.

Feeny Jonson, K. 1997. *The New Elementary Teacher's Handbook: (Almost) Everything You Need to Know for Your First Years of Teaching.* Corwin Press.

Filardo, F. 1998. *Primer for the Beginning Teacher.* Prior Press of Lakewod Inc.

Gaither, J. 1998. *A Survival Kit for Substitutes and New Teachers.* Jenrod Publishing Co.

Harmin, M. 1995. I*nspiring Discipline: A Practical Guide for Today's Classroom.* Washington DC: National Education Association.

Kimeldorf, M. 1993. *Educator's Job Search: The Ultimate Guide to Finding Positions in Education.* Washington DC: National Education Association.

Kosler, K. 1998. *The Discipline Checklist: Advice from 60 Successful Elementary Teachers.* Washington DC: National Education Association.

Kohn, A. 1999. *The Schools Our Children Deserve: Moving Beyond Traditional Classrooms and "Tougher Standards."* Houghton Mifflin Co.

Kraut, H. 1997. *Teaching and the Art of Successful Classroom Management: A How-to Guidebook for Teachers in Secondary Schools*, 2nd ed. Washington DC: National Education Association.

Lysons, N. 1998. *With Portfolio in Hand: Validating the New Teacher Professionalism.* Teachers College Press.

McDonald, E.S. and Hershman, D.M. 1998. *Survival Kit for New Teachers.* Inspiring Teachers Publishing Group.

Morey, A. I and Murphy, D. 1990. *Designing Programs for New Teachers: The California Experience.* Wested.

Murray, B.A. and Murray, K.T. 1997. *Pitfalls and Potholes: A Checklist for Avoiding Common Mistakes of Beginning Teachers.* Washington DC: National Education Association.

Nathan, M. 1995. *The New Teacher's Survival Guide.* Styhis Publishing.

Orange, C. 2000. *25 Biggest Mistakes a Teacher Makes and How to Avoid Them.* Thousand Oaks, CA: Corwin Press Inc.

Pelletier, C.A. 1999. *Strategies for Successful Student Teaching: A Comprehensive Guide*. Needham Heights, MA: Allyn & Bacon.

Quarles, A. 1991. *Classroom Clout: Empowering the New and Veteran Teacher of Today*. Linton Day Publishing Co.

Reiff, J.C. 1992. *Learning Styles*. Washington DC: National Education Association.

Remy, M.N. 1997. *A New Teacher's Survival Guide: Everything They Forgot to Tell You during Credentialing*. Siena Publishing.

Reyes, R. 1991. *The Ten Commandments for Teaching*. Washington DC: National Education Association.

Reynolds, M.C. 1989. *Knowledge Base for the Beginning Teacher*. Pergamon Press.

Schell, L.M. and Burden, P. 1992. *Countdown to the First Day of School*. Washington DC: National Education Association.

Staff of Canter. 1998. *First-Class Teacher: Success Strategies for New Teachers*. Lee Canters Association.

Tickle, L. 1994. *The Induction of New Teachers: Reflective Professional Practice* (Teacher Development). Cassell Academic.

Tubbs, N. 1996. *The New Teacher: An Introduction to Teaching in Comprehensive Education* (Quality in Secondary Schools and College Services). David Fulton Publishing.

Wertz, J.E. 1999. *Making Science Cool: Strategies for Changing Student's Negative Attitudes Toward Science*. Washington DC: National Education Association.

Videos

Active Learning. VHS, 1992. Washington DC: NEA Professional Library Video.

Teaching Teachers. VHS, 1995. Teacher TV episode 41. Washington DC: NEA Professional Library Video.

The Art of Learning. VHS, 1993. Washington DC: NEA Professional Library Video.

The Making of a Teacher. VHS, 1992. Episode 2. Washington DC: NEA Professional Library Video.

Web Sites

Advice for educators teaching the English language can be found at http://www.catesol.org

New research-based resources for mathematics and sciences are easily accessible at http://www.wcer.wisc.edu/ncisla

The National Center for Postsecondary Teaching, Learning and Assessment researches curriculum programs, faculty and instruction, out-of-class programs, and organization structures and policies. The results of this research are available for purchase at http://www.ed/psu/edu/cshe/htdocs/research/NCTLA/nctla.htm

Everybody wants free goodies and you can get them at http://www.eyesoftime.com/teacher/index.htm

Additional teaching supplies for the classroom can be found at http://www.reallygoodstuff.com

Find 70 years of experience in Becker's school supplies online catalog at http://www.shopbecker.com/

In need of teaching supplies, curriculum materials or learning aids? They are available at http://www.school-tools.com/

It really is a small world thanks to the technological advances of the Internet. Why not introduce your students to the World Wide Web at http://integratingtheinternet.com/index/index5.html

Need a film to supplement your lesson plans? Or perhaps you need a movie to catch you up on current teaching issues. Both types of educational cinema are for sale at http://www.films.com

If you need something to entertain your students during another rainy day lunch, try an educational video available at http://www.classroomvideos.com

Having trouble creating a lesson plan for this week's curriculum? Grab some ideas from http://www.the-gateway.org

Does your curriculum need a boost? Gain fresh ideas from http://www.teacher2teacher.com

To gain resources and support as a new teacher, visit http://www.new-teacher.com

Advice for teacher by teachers is available on this chatboard at http://www.teachers.net/mentors/classroom_management

Find ideas for new and experienced elementary school teachers at http://www.ametro.net

Share adventures with other teachers who have a passion for teaching at http://www.soulteacher.com

Journals/Magazines

Jehlen, A. "Who's the Mentor?" *NEA Today*, March 2000, 8-9.

"Lifeline to City Schools: New Teachers Stick with Tough City Assignments with the Help of Veteran Peers." *NEA Today*, March 1999, 21.

"Teaching Future Teachers." *NEA Today*, January 1999, 21.

"Stats for Survival: Take a Closer Look at Teaching Opportunities and Conditions." *Tomorrow's Teachers*, 2000 ed.: 25-29.

Merina, A. "Teaching Tolerance." *Tomorrow's Teachers*, 1997 ed.: 10.

For up-to-date information on current educational issues, access this online quarterly journal at http://www.newhorizons.org/newslarchive.html

Can't find the information you're looking for? Look at more than 400 journals in this annotated bibliography, http://cimc.education.wisc.edu/resources/anno_AB.html

Organizations

DELTA (Design for Excellence: Linking Teachers and Achievement)
c/o Carol Barnes, Executive Director
350 South Bixel Street Suite 295
Los Angeles, CA 90017
They provide professional development and a support system for aspiring and beginning teachers in Southern California.

Full Circle Institute
3318 Hennepin Avenue South
Minneapolis, MN 55408
The Full Circle Institute adopts classrooms and provides them with full curriculum and lesson plans about science and preserving the environment.

National Education Association
1201 16th Street NW
Washington, DC 20036
The NEA is a powerful link to teachers across the nation. Its publications provide teachers with up-to-date information on education issues and teaching techniques.

NCTE (National Council of Teachers of English) - **TEACH2000**
Contact Melanie Marker
800-369-6283 ext. 3660
mmarker@ncte.org
TEACH2000 reaches out to educators who started teaching between the summer of 1999 and the summer of 2000. These first-time teachers are eligible for a free NCTE membership, free NCTE journal, magazine subscriptions, mentorship support, book and conference discounts, and online resources.

Ten Sigma
1610 Commerce Drive
PO Box 846
Mankato, MN 56002-0846
Ten Sigma is a nonprofit organization that develops practical materials and training programs for new teachers.

TESOL (Teachers of English to Speakers of Other Languages)
700 S. Washington Street Suite 200
Alexandria, VA 22314
TESOL is a national organization that advances professional preparation for dealing with non-English speaking students. It links groups of educators worldwide and enhances their communication.

Voyager Expanded Learning
1125 Longpoint Avenue
Dallas, Texas 75247
This is a national education reform initiative that provides learning programs and teacher training for public schools.

"Real teachers consider their teaching a gift they give to their students—a gift that can change the course of their students' lives forever."

Patti Ralabate